GUINNESS

TURF ACCOUNTS

Graham Sharpe
Illustrations by David Arthur

GUINNESS PUBLISHING

This book is dedicated to, as the song almost said, the ones I love . . .

Editor: Charles Richards
Design and Layout: Michael Morey

Published in Great Britain by Guinness Publishing Ltd,
33 London Road, Enfield, Middlesex

Typeset in Century Old Style
by Ace Filmsetting Ltd, Frome, Somerset

Printed and bound in Great Britain by The Bath Press, Bath

British Library Cataloguing in Publication Data
Sharpe, Graham
Turf accounts.
1. Racehorses. Racing
I. Title
798.4
ISBN 0-85112-393-7

Here is the author vowing to have absolutely nothing to do with racing horses ever again. Hardly surprising, really, as he had just spent the best part of four hours competing in the gruelling William Hill Man versus Horse Marathon, failing dismally to defeat any of his four-legged rivals and being ignominiously outpaced on the final run-in by a four-year-old boy who had strayed on to the course!

Three racehorses have played a major part in the life of Graham Sharpe. The first was called Baulking Green. He raced in the early sixties and won countless hunter chases, convincing the gullible Sharpe that backing winners was just a matter of 'putting it down and picking it up'.

What the fledgling punter had failed to realise, of course, was that Baulking Green was a phenomenal horse racing aginst moderate rivals, and that a small stake on the horse every time he ran would never produce a large enough profit to justify early retirement!

Sea Pigeon was the next horse to loom large in the life of G.S. Though finishing a modest seventh in the Derby, the Pigeon went on to become that rare phenomenon, a legend in his own lifetime, winning two Champion Hurdles and countless other top quality races both on the flat and over the jumps, endearing himself to a certain Mr Sharpe in the process.

Finally, on the very day of the birth of the first son gifted to Graham and his wife Sheila, a horse called Sharpo took part in the William Hill Sprint Championship at York. Noticing the coincidence between his greeting to the new-born son ('Hello, Sharpo') and the name of this relatively unknown sprinter, Graham rushed to back his son's namesake, who went on to prove himself the best sprinter of the early eighties and, in the process, to line the pockets of the Sharpe dynasty!

Since then Sharpe has confined himself to writing about and quoting the odds on horses in his capacity as Media Relations Manager for William Hill. But should anyone ever be rash enough to name their horse Luton Town FC, be assured that the Sharpe family fortunes will be riding on its back every time it races!

CONTENTS

SUPERSTITIONS AND RITUALS

Horse racing is chock-full of superstitions, many of them extremely personal to the people involved – but very few of them, strangely, seem to be given much credence by the horses themselves!

Many punters apparently believe it is an omen of good luck to meet a cross-eyed woman on the way to the races, or that a pin from a wedding dress will readily pin-point a winner. Jockeys are said to consider it unlucky to drop their whips before a race, to stand their riding boots on the floor or not to be addressed by name before a race. All parties are, so the story goes, convinced that to kiss a horse after it has just won a race ensures good luck for the future.

Trainer Bill Watts sets the standard for the rest in the racing world, admitting to at least half a dozen pet superstitions. 'I won't wear any blue on a racecourse. Red is lucky. I won't pass salt from hand to hand. If I see a funeral, that's the end of the day's proceedings. Weddings are lucky. If something goes terribly wrong in the morning it never goes right in the afternoon.'

Jockey Sharon Murgatroyd was preparing to ride Great Gusto at Ripon in June 1989, when a gallant racegoer came up to her and handed her some lavender for luck. She carried the lavender in her glove and won the race at odds of 20–1.

The Green Party may be making ground in the political world – but they are unlikely to recruit many members from the racing scene. Champion trainer Henry Cecil says, 'I hate green. Most of my family have died in green and I never wear

anything of that colour. One great ancestor fell down the stairs when wearing green and another died eating watercress which is green.' Former champion flat jockey Willie Carson is another green-hater, while former champion jump jockey Ron Barry claims, 'As a rider I did all the usual things – like trying to avoid riding for owners with green colours. Even now I won't let my wife Liz go out in a green coat.'

Weddings and funerals bring out the best in superstitious trainers Peter Walwyn and Mark Tompkins, but their rituals are very different. Walwyn maintains that 'if I see a funeral I have to see the coffin, and if I pass a wedding I must see the bride', but Tompkins does not escape so lightly. If he sees a funeral he insists on holding his collar until he spots a dog and warns that 'if you see a wedding and catch sight of the bride, you might as well go home. I always shut my eyes when I go past a wedding.'

Magpies inevitably receive a lot of attention, especially, it would seem, from trainers. Ginger McCain (of Red Rum fame) says Good Morning to the first one he sees, while one is never enough for David Elsworth (Desert Orchid): 'If I ever see one I am always looking for the other. One is supposed to be unlucky, but if you see two it is good.' Nicky Henderson (See You Then) doesn't like the colour green or magpies (what would he do if he saw a green magpie!), and Jack Berry (O I Oyston) positively hates magpies. 'When I go racing I have to travel six miles before getting on to the motorway. If I don't see a magpie before the motorway I am OK,' he says.

There are superstitions about horses, too, and a well known example referring to those with white feet, runs as follows:
One white foot, buy a horse,
Two white feet, try a horse,
Three white feet, look well about him,
Four white feet, do well without him.

For over 30 years Kentucky Oaks-winning owners were delighted with the silver cups they received as a memento of their fillies' triumph – until 1984 when Leslie Combs II declared that the horseshoe motif on the cups, awarded since 1951, was pointing downward and therefore 'making the luck run out'. Officials agreed with Combs (who was not too superstitious to have named his filly Lucky Lucky Lucky) and they had the manufacturer turn the horseshoe 180 degrees to point upward.

Even the greatest have their superstitions. Sir Gordon Richards would always raise his hat to a chimney sweep on the way to the races, and liked to wear the same tie and braces on big race days.

Trainer David Nicholson was heard to remark, 'I guarantee that what I wore at last season's Gold Cup I will wear again this year.' But then a victorious trainer (in 1988 with Charter Party) would!

The right outfit is important to Ron Barry, too. 'We always trample new racing silks on the floor and get them a little dirty,' he says. Especially if they happen to be green, no doubt!

After riding Well To Do to win the 1972 Grand National, jockey Graham Thorner insisted on wearing the same pair of underpants every time he raced. Said fellow jump jockey Richard Pitman, 'He wore them until there was nothing left of them, just a bit of elastic round his legs. He even had to keep them on with another pair! But there was no way he'd ride without them.' As for Pitman, his only superstition when riding was always to put his right boot on first.

After it was carried into second place in the Irish Derby in 1983 by Carlingford Castle, owner Frank Roe, President of the Irish Circuit Court, always insisted that riders of his Flat horses should wear his jumping jersey instead of more usual silks. He was only persuaded to relent when one of them told him that the jersey soaked up so much sweat that it increased the weight being carried by his horses.

Owner, steward and Jockey Club member Edward John Stanley, the 18th Earl of Derby, confessed that his superstitions include never sitting down to dinner with thirteen people at the table, but one of his predecessors, the 12th Earl (who owned Sir Peter Teazle, the 1787 Derby winner), had a rather odder superstition - he thought pianos were unlucky and refused to have one in his home. In fact, if he came across one anywhere else he would lock it up and throw away the key.

Jockey Eddie Hide, who finished his riding career in 1985, was always rather wary of the number 13. He rode his last winner on August 13, 1985 and broke his leg at York one Friday the 13th. However, when Morston was Eddie's 13th Derby ride and was number 13 on the card, he won the race.

Jockey John Lowe has a 'numbers' superstition: 'If I am drawn seven or on a horse number seven it makes me feel that I have a better chance, and my car must have a seven in its number plate.'

Henry Cecil has a peculiar superstition which he confessed to the *Sporting Life*. 'When I go racing I always fill up the car with petrol on the way there. If I don't fill it up I don't win. Even if it is a question of just putting a quarter of a gallon in I will always stop at a garage on the way, otherwise the whole day's racing is a disaster.'

Jockey-turned-commentator Jimmy Lindley is another racing man who will never pass the salt.

Trainer Alex Whiting's Great Uncle Cyril predicted with his dying breath that no descendant of his would ever win a race at Nottingham. Whiting has made over 30 attempts to prove his Great Uncle wrong – without success. Although it is known that Uncle Cyril's ashes were scattered on the course, it is not known precisely why he made his prediction. But it has resisted all attempts to overcome it – Whiting even called in a priest to exorcise Great Uncle Cyril's ghost, but all in vain. Even when Whiting's Taylor's Renovation was in front approaching the finishing line, the jockey suddenly tumbled off the horse!

The ghost of Fred Archer, champion jockey for the last of 13 consecutive times in 1886, is said to haunt Newmarket Heath. He shot himself at the age of 29 and a famous print of Archer on a grey horse galloping across the Heath is accompanied by a verse saying, 'Across the heath, along the course/Tis said upon a phantom horse/The greatest jockey of our days/Rides nightly in the moonlight rays.' And perhaps there is something in the tales because in 1987 the *Sunday Sport* newspaper employed psychic Doris Balwark to pass on to readers tips from beyond the grave purporting to come from Archer.

Colonel William Hall-Walker, whose bloodstock breeding enterprise of the early 20th century eventually led to the founding of the Irish National Stud, had an unusual theory about breeding. Hall-Walker would match his mares and stallions according to their astrological zodiac signs. He had a horoscope cast for every foal and if it proved unfavourable then the horse had to go. This was the case with Prince Palatine - who went on to win the St Leger and the Ascot Gold Cup.

Desperate for rain to encourage grass to grow over ground left barren by drainage work, Uttoxeter racecourse called in a Red Indian rain-man during the hot, dry summer of 1989. The drainage had been installed to try to beat the problem of waterlogging at the course, but when the grass didn't grow back, medicine man Tosu was called in. A racecourse spokesman told the *Daily Mirror*, 'If Tosu does the trick we'll use him regularly - but we'll stop short of a totem pole at the winning post.' Within 48 hours, rain was pouring down.

Jump jockey Phil Tuck was once regarded as the most superstitious rider in the game - he would salute magpies on the way to the races, in fact he even named his house The Magpies and painted it black and white. He would always wear the same holey socks, use the same pin and wear the same tattered T-shirt. Finally, towards the end of 1988 Tuck took stock and decided to dump the superstitions. 'It was getting out of hand. Everyone was on about it all the time. I suddenly thought, it's all daftness. I suppose I've grown up, really.'

The last word on superstitions must go to trainer Henry Candy, as superstitious as most and more so than many: 'Magpies, funerals, black cats, trains going over bridges etc, all receive plenty of attention in the full knowledge that it is all rubbish.'

HORSES' TALES

All thoroughbreds are descended from one of three stallions - The Byerley Turk, The Darley Arabian or The Godolphin Arabian.

The first horse to travel by horse-box to a major race was Elis, a well fancied candidate for the 1836 St Leger. His owner, Lord George Bentinck was keen to get good odds so he made it known that the horse was still at Goodwood shortly before the race. In those days horses were generally walked to the course. Naturally it was assumed that Elis would be unable to get to Doncaster in time for the race so his odds drifted. However, Bentinck's groom, John Doe, had come up with the idea for a horse-drawn wagon to transport Elis in. The horse duly arrived at Doncaster in good time and in excellent shape and he obliged in the big race. The idea soon caught on in a big way.

The first foreign bred horse to win a major English race was Prioress, the American winner of the 1857 Cesarewitch.

Miss Nightingale secured an unwanted place in racing history by being the victim of the first recorded case of a horse being 'got at' before a big race. The filly was engaged in a race which she was expected to win in 1778, but was found dead in her box shortly before the race. She had two pounds of duck-shot in her intestines, it was later discovered.

Tagalie has a place in history - she's the only grey filly to win the Derby, in 1912.

Archer walked the 550 miles from his stable in New South Wales, to win the first running of the Melbourne Cup in 1861.

The most famous case of a horse being kidnapped was Derby winner Shergar in 1983 - a £2 million ransom was demanded at one stage but the horse was never recovered. In 1975 American mare Fanfreluche was taken from her paddock in Kentucky but was later found safe in a field and in 1974 Italian terrorists kidnapped Nelson Bunker Hunt's Carnauba. The owner refused ransom demands and the horse was finally recovered alive from a knacker's yard.

The first horse to be flown to a race meeting was El Lobo in October 1946, and he duly obliged by winning a handicap at Bay Meadows, San

Francisco. The pilot of the plane, Major William Hucke, cleaned up by backing the horse.

His racecourse performances guaranteed Preakness a place in turf history – three years after he won the first stakes race run at Pimlico Racecourse, USA, in 1870, the Maryland Jockey Club honoured the colt by naming a race in his honour. That race became part of the coveted American Triple Crown, but Preakness' future wasn't so bright. The horse was sent to stud at the Duke of Hamilton's in England. The horse's temper was bad but not as bad as the Duke's who finally shot Preakness in a fit of anger.

In 1924 a horse called Black Gold became the only Kentucky Derby winner to also win the Ohio Derby at Thistledown, Ohio. The horse was owned by Rosa M Hoots who always insisted on being paid prize money in cash, and trained by Oklahoma Indian Hedley 'Three Fingered' Webb who apparently never uttered a word.

Black Gold failed at stud and returned to racing – but in his first race back he broke a leg at the Fair Grounds course in New Orleans and was buried right where he fell on the infield.

Russian horse Gazolit raced as a three-year-old in the early 1980s even though his father had died in 1975 – for Gazolit was one of, if not the first test-tube thoroughbred racehorses, conceived through artificial insemination. Gazolit's dam, Gana, was fertilised with sperm taken from the great Russian champion, Anilin. Horses conceived in this way are not permitted to race in the West.

Comparing horses of different generations is virtually impossible, but there is almost unanimous agreement that the finest chaser of all was Arkle, the triple Cheltenham Gold Cup winner. Respected judges at Timeform said in 1966 that Arkle had proved himself 'the greatest chaser ever' and have not needed to revise that opinion since. Timeform's highest-rated Flat horse is 1965 Derby winner Sea Bird.

The speeds at which racehorses run races seem to have changed little over the last century. However, over the same period of time human athletic achievements have improved dramatically. Professor William Hill of Edinburgh University who specialises in Animal Genetics set out to investigate. He found that in 1850 the ten year average winning time for the Derby was 176 seconds which, by 1910 had improved to 159 seconds but since then had remained virtually the same. The St Leger revealed a similar pattern. Said Professor Hill, 'I think the solution to the mystery is that there has been no improvement in the gene pool. There are too few stallions for breeding.'

Researchers at New York's Cornell University in 1989 came up with an unusual explanation for temperamental behaviour by racehorses – fear of the dark. After observing that horses kept in a windowless barn would switch on a light by repeatedly walking through the beam of a photo-electric cell, they concluded, 'The new findings may have a practical impact on racegoers as well as affecting horse owners. Racehorses are notoriously temperamental, so punters may do well to check if their favourites sleep with a night light.'

After competing in the Cheltenham Gold Cup, the Grand National and the Maryland Cup, Casamayor faced an entirely new challenge when his trainer John Bentley gave him to the Metropolitan Police in 1984, at which time he was 13 years old. The horse later did duty during the riots outside the Wapping headquarters of Rupert Murdoch's newspaper empire when printers were picketing. Casamayor was based at Hyde Park Police Station and his rider PC Peter Lennol said, 'You would think that with his kind of breeding he would be a bit of a prima donna but on the contrary he is calm and disciplined.'

Sheila's Cottage won the 1948 Grand National - but showed precious little gratitude to her jockey, Arthur Thompson. When he visited her after the race she bit off the top of his finger.

In his build-up to three gallant attempts to win the Whitbread Gold Cup, top chaser Mandarin was partly trained on Mackeson, brewed by the race's sponsor. Mandarin was runner up in three consecutive years. As a consolation, after his third near miss in 1960, Colonel Bill Whitbread awarded the popular jumper two free bottles of Mackeson per day - delivered to his stable from a nearby Lambourn pub.

Melody Town, stable lass for trainer Alan Bailey, was at Goodwood in August 1989, to lead the stable's entry for the Oakley Handicap, Cotton On Quick, round the parade ring. While she was doing this, trainer Sue Armytage, saddling Damaskeen in the race, discovered that her jockey, Dewi Williams, wasn't qualified to ride. Melody was quickly called in as substitute jockey - and she and Damaskeen duly won by half a length. Damaskeen was also Sue Armytage's first winner on the Flat.

At the peak of his powers, Irish races for which the great Arkle was entered were handicapped twice - once assuming he ran, and again assuming he didn't.

Horses often pal up with other creatures and pine if they are separated from them. The great French mare Allez France was friendly with a sheep, and 1933 Oaks winner Chatelaine had one thing in common with shock 100-1 Grand National winner Foinavon - they both doted on a goat. Irish chaser Sunnyhill went everywhere with a goose while 1929 National winner Gregalach couldn't be torn away from a terrier. The Godolphin Arabian, one of the founding sires of all thoroughbreds, doted on a stable cat.

Poor jumper Elsich was probably the worst horse ever to race in Britain. After fifty failures the authorities finally stepped in to refuse to accept any further entries for the horse. This was in June 1947 and by then Elsich had completed the course in only a third of his starts. He began his racing career at the age of nine in February 1945, falling twice in two different races at Cheltenham on the same day. His owner-trainer Charles Edwards maintained a high opinion of the horse who ran out, fell and was pulled up in the Cheltenham Gold Cup and fell at the first in the National. The gelding did manage a second place once - a distance behind his solitary opponent.

Thoroughbred horse Charper, from Britain, came out on top in an 1825 race between two Cossack horses and two thoroughbreds, held near St Petersburg. Charper's win led to many more thoroughbreds being imported to Russia with the result that organised racing became a more frequent occurrence there.

Huntress Grace ran in two hurdle races on the same day at Fakenham in May 1983, but was pulled up in both. Exactly five years later, on the same date, May 30, Silver Snow also ran in two hurdles races at Fakenham - faring somewhat better, winning one of the races and finishing third in the other.

Two-year-old filly St Wendred was the first horse to race for the Church of England. In 1986 she was given for a year to the parish of St Martin's, Exning, near Newmarket by a local trainer. The horse raced in the colours used for altar dressing - red, purple, green and white - and Rev Cedric Catton, registered as her owner, said, 'I think you can say that we will be supporting her in the usual way.' However, the collections weren't boosted by much, she finished last on her debut and was never a world beater.

Racing for home on Mountain Kingdom in the 1989 Ormonde Stakes at Chester, Steve Cauthen felt one of his rivals snapping at his heels - literally. For Lazaz, in second place, took a bite at Cauthen's boot as they thundered up the finishing straight. Cauthen commented afterwards, 'I thought it was more playful than savage.'

A horse with a sweet tooth can prove expensive for his owner. No Bombs in 1979 and De Rigueur in 1987 were both disqualified after winning races when a prohibited substance, theobromine, was found. Both had eaten a Mars bar before their races.

Puerto Rican horse Galgo Jr set a record by winning 137 races between 1930 and 1936. In 1931 he had set another record by winning 30 times in one season.

Dr Syntax won the Preston Gold Cup in seven consecutive years from 1815 to 1821, a feat never equalled in any other race.

George De Mar, an American horse, was probably the busiest horse ever to race, appearing 333 times in the mid-1920s. John Jay S raced a record 76 times in America in 1890.

No horse ever raced at an older age than Creggmore Boy, 22 when finishing 4th in 1962 at Cartmel.

A horse called Sweetest When She's Naked won two races on the same day at a meeting in Leith, Scotland in April 1760.

1864 Oaks winner Fille de l'Air had to be escorted to the winners' enclosure by a specially hired group of prize fighters. This followed the filly's controversial failure in the 2000 Guineas for which she was favourite. One racing correspondent, Harkaway, wrote, 'I think a grosser robbery was never perpetrated upon the turf.' Suspicion fell on the horse's owner, Frenchman Count de Lagrange, jockey Arthur Edwards and trainer Tom Jennings. Edwards was probably the guilty party and was lucky to escape with his life, but was apparently unrepentant and it was strongly suspected that he was up to his tricks again with the same horse when Fille de l'Air finished third in the Grand Prix de Paris and Edwards 'forgot' to weigh in after the race.

The first racehorse drawn by great equine artist J F Herring was 1815 St Leger winner Filho da Puta - which is Portuguese for 'son of a whore'!

Horses' names can no longer be changed once they have been entered in a race or registered in the General Stud Book - but this was not always the case. In 1786 a horse known as the Paymaster colt won the St Leger. Next time out he raced at Newcastle under the name St Leger and a month later he reappeared at Carlisle as Paragon.

In 1791 the King Fergus colt who won the St Leger later became Young Traveller and then Lauderdale. The 1776 St Leger winner had no name at all until fifty years later when historian John Orton decided that the first winner of the oldest Classic should not just be known as 'the Sampson filly' so he dubbed her Allabaculla, which seems to have stuck. More recently the 1947 champion two-year-old, Lerins, reappeared for the next season known as My Babu, under which name he won the 2000 Guineas.

Names nowadays must consist of no more than eighteen letters and spaces. Many people think using horse names to plug a commercial product is a recent innovation, but as long ago as 1898 Celladema Embrocation and Celladema Ointment ran and won over jumps thus boosting the perceived efficacy of those medicinal items.

The two horses taking part in a 1000 crown-a-side race between two French noblemen in 1641 'enjoyed' an unorthodox preparation - both the Prince d'Harcourt's mount and that of the Duc de Joyeuse were fed on bread made with beans and aniseed and, for two days before the race, each given between 200 and 300 fresh eggs. The Duc's horse won.

Seattle Dancer cost a record $13.1 million in 1985. His career lasted from April 18–June 28, 1987 during which time he won two of his five starts.

At least 4300 punters backed Music Review every time the horse ran - for owner John Beynon invited all the members of his Coronet Bingo Club to back his sprinter whenever it ran. If the horse won they were quids in but if it lost they could use their losing betting slips to get free admission to the Bingo Club.

In 1969 Ribofilio started favourite for the 2000 Guineas, The Derby, The Irish Derby and the St Leger - and was beaten in all four.

Lottery was such an outstanding steeplechaser that in his heyday during the 1840s, races were framed with the condition 'open to all horses - except Lottery' in order to deliberately discourage him from competing or entering.

Cloudy View won six races in nine days during the 1952–53 New Zealand season - scoring two wins each at Oamaru, Kurow and Kumara.

Black Lad was certainly the most 'six-essful' horse in training when he won two races on the same day at Taumarunui, New Zealand, in July 1957 - the winning dividends for the two races were six pounds sixteen shillings and sixpence, and six pounds six shillings and sixpence.

Worthless as a racehorse - she won one small selling race at Windsor in 1985 - Fort Duchesny was sold for just 1500 Guineas to David Morley, who looks after polo ponies at Cowdray Park in Sussex. Within three years Fort Duchesny had become the best polo pony in England, was partnered by top player Carlos Gracida, and attracted a rejected bid of £300,000.

Turn of the century wonder horse from New Zealand, Carbine, could never be described as 'wet behind the ears'; for the great champion hated getting his ears wet, so much so that on one wet big-race day his trainer had to walk all the way to the start carrying an umbrella over the horse's head. He finally raced with ear plugs attached to his bridle.

Gold Man was down to run in a jump race at Avondale, New Zealand in July 1948. Shortly before the race his trainer, G Walker, was injured and taken to hospital. A lad who didn't know Gold Man was directed to the stables to saddle him up for the race, but he saddled up the similar looking Peria Chief - who had never jumped a fence in his life. The race was off before the mistake was realised - Peria Chief jumped round unscathed - but the comments of his jockey upon discovering what had happened are, perhaps fortunately, not recorded.

They bred 'em tough in 1883. Sir Modred won three races in three days at Riccarton, New Zealand, and after the third, his trainer, Edward Cutts, sent him back to the stable for a well-earned issue of bran and water. Sir Modred wolfed down the food and drink before word came back to the stable that the owner wanted Sir Modred saddled up for a half-mile race later that afternoon. Despite the trainer's protests the horse had to return to race again - and he won.

Coincidence backers must have had a field day on Derby day in 1874. The race was won at odds of 9–1 by George Frederick - on the ninth birthday of Prince George Frederick. In 1989 the Wonderfuel Gas Handicap at Chester was won by Burnt Fingers, and there can have been few better backed 'coincidence' winners than Royal Mark, who won the Wedding Handicap Chase at Windsor on 14 November 1973 – the day Princess Anne wed Captain Mark Phillips.

Two of the runners on November 18 1988 were literally a dead loss. We're In The Money, having been officially listed as dead two days earlier, ran fourth in a Novice Hurdle at Ascot while on the same day English River, listed as dead in the form book, contested a race at Nottingham.

One can only wonder at the origin of the horse who won a 1774 race at Chester – 'Mine Ass-in-a-Band Box' owned by a Mr Boyd.

Many people were intrigued by the name of that useful hurdler, Kybo, until owner Isidore Kerman explained that it was an acronym of the advice often given to him by his mother 'Keep your bowels open'.

Jack-Berry-trained racehorse O I Oyston helped raise money for charity when in August 1989 he was released into a field which was divided into hundreds of squares, each of which had been sold off, to leave his droppings in the winning square. O I Oyston kept enthusiastic spectators waiting for forty minutes before picking a winner, and winning ticket-holder Bob Heathcote donated the £1000 prize to the Royal Manchester Children's Hospital.

Ratepayer David Preston, of Elmbridge, wrote to his local Town Clerk requesting that popular Gold Cup winner Desert Orchid should be made a Freeman of Elmbridge for his exploits at the Borough's Sandown track. The request had to be turned down eventually as, reported Town Clerk David Jenkins, 'Only a human being can be made a Freeman.'

Birmingham, winner of the 1830 St Leger, took an unusual fancy to his owner's wife, whom he would follow around the house like a pet dog.

Panegyrist was nothing if not persistent. The horse finally got his head in front at the age of 14 after 38 unsuccessful attempts, in a small race at Ayr in March 1989. Commented jockey Joe O'Gorman, 'He'll be useful if they give him a bit of time.'

The courage of some horses is often doubted by spectators at race-courses – but jockey Wesley Ward is convinced that his mount Sezincote was literally dying to win a race at Arlington International, Lexington, USA on July 4, 1989. Sezincote, a three-year-old, was out to land a third consecutive victory, and did so, before collapsing and dying one hundred yards after the finish line. 'The horse had more desire to win than to save his own life,' said Ward. 'I could feel him starting to hurt at the eighth pole. He came down hard on his left knee. I started to take a good hold of him – I was trying to hold him up. I'm sure he knew where the wire was. And just as we passed it, I knew he was going to go down. I jumped off as fast as I could to avoid getting crushed. I could see he was going to die soon, I bent down and petted his head. Then I saw his eyes roll backwards.' Probable cause of Sezincote's death was a ruptured blood vessel or heart attack.

Active during 1987, Commonsidr Gypsy came across his unusual name by accident, explained part owner Leslie May, revealing that the horse was supposed to have been registered as Commonside Gypsy, after Commonside in Sheffield which is where Leslie has a pub. The mistake occurred during transmission of the name, 'We decided to let the name stand but it caused more confusion than we had bargained for,' said Leslie.

Canebora, a rather ordinary looking colt, will be remembered as more than Canada's 1963 Horse of the Year and second winner of the Triple Crown in that country. The brown colt, the last Canadian-bred to win the coveted tri-cornered gold trophy, was also something of a music critic! In fact, Canebora's ear for a horn caused The Ontario Jockey Club to cease its traditional trumpeted 'Call To The Post' for runners. Canebora, you see, went berserk in the paddock every time he so much as heard the first toot of the trumpet. Canebora had the misfortune of being stabled, as a youngster, at the military Fort Erie next to the area where a new bugler was being trained. The bugler was proficient enough, but not on horseback. So every evening the would-be-bugler saddled up, then rode his pony up and down the dirt road practising his routine. Unfortunately, Canebora's stall was closest to the well-meaning bugler. Canebora was a model of decorum in every way. Until, of course, he heard the first sounds of brass in the paddock. Then he became a raging bull. Finally, after several fits of temper, trainer Gord (Pete) McCann figured out the problem. The order went out. No Music, please, when Canebora's in the paddock. That did the trick, and Canebora thrived on the silence.

The 1863 Lanark Silver Bell was won by a horse called Dick Swiveller.

The two-year-old Stetchworth literally raced like a shot when winning a race at Redcar in 1978. Partnered by jockey Taffy Thomas, the horse suddenly reared up and veered towards the rails just as the runners came under orders. Thomas was almost thrown out of the saddle, but he managed to stay on and he and Stetchworth won the race by half a length. After the race, gun-shot marks were found on the colt's rump - and it later transpired that three youths hiding in long grass had taken pot shots at runners in the race.

King's Kestrel cost a quarter of a million pounds as a yearling - great things were expected of him. But he proved to be useless. When Somerset cricket skipper Roy Kerslake sent him to be trained by all-conquering Martin Pipe, not even that record breaker could conjure a win out of the wayward animal, who would insist on pulling himself up half way through a race. When last heard of as a seven year-old he was 'working' at Gaunts Riding Stables in Somerset and being trained as a show-jumper.

Monksfield, who won the Champion Hurdle in 1978 and '79 was returned at odds of 647-1 on the Tote when he won the first race of his career, on the Flat as a two-year-old.

After winning the 1977 Champion Hurdle on Night Nurse, his jockey Paddy Broderick announced that he would no longer ride over fences in order to avoid injuring himself and being unable to ride Night Nurse. Later that year in the Christmas Hurdle at Kempton on Boxing Day Broderick's career was terminated when he and Night Nurse fell.

Students from Widnes Sixth Form College were blamed for damaging the stuffed remains of great racehorse Brown Jack, standing at the Stable Grill, Widnes, but found at Christmas, 1986, lying on the ground - minus an ear.

A huge gamble on Zusrab throughout Australia in December 1988 saw the horse's odds in the Savoir Handicap at Moonee Valley, Melbourne plunge from 100-1 to 6-1 as bookies' liabilities reached over two million Aussie dollars. Zusrab finished second, beaten by inches.

1967 Champion Hurdle winner Saucy Kit finally passed away in 1980 at the Blakeley Stud, managed by his former jockey Roy Edwards, who explained, 'He was a super horse and loved grey mares. He was covering a grey one day when he rolled off dead - and she got in foal!'

Harvey Wallbanger is a very useful performer - he's won over twenty races in the USA, usually running over sprint distances. Ten-year-old Harvey has a special racing diet - a half bale of alfalfa grass and between three and five gallons of sweet oats a day, and his ideal racing weight is 1600 lbs. Harvey Wallbanger is a buffalo, but he is more than capable of beating the racehorses who take him on throughout the States. Harvey has so far only raced against American quarter bred horses and English trainer Jack Berry reckons that 'any decent racehorse bred for sprinting would be able to beat a buffalo' - and Berry has challenged Harvey's owner, 33 year-old T C Thorstenson of Wyoming, 'Bring your fellah over to Hamilton Park and I'll take him on with one of my horses - and we'll win.'

The name of the legendary Australian horse, Phar Lap, is Javanese - they are the words to describe forked lightning, literally, 'the wink of the skies'.

Grey horses are not an uncommon sight on racecourses - but pure white runners are rare indeed. In the last 25 years just three have raced in Britain - in 1966 Mont Blanc was twice a winner as a three-year-old, trained by Walter Nightingall, then White Wonder, who ended his career in the late seventies, won eight races for Paul Cole and Harry Blackshaw. White Wonder was actually sired by Mont Blanc. In 1989 Bill Stubbs trained a white two-year-old, Comtich.

The ghost of 1876 Derby winner Kisber is reputed to haunt the Parhassy Castle in Germany where he died at the age of 18. Sightings report that Kisber, ridden by a jockey clad in crimson, emerald and white (the colours carried by the horse when racing), is seen hurtling along flat out, intent on re-winning the Derby.

'The boy's grave', near Newmarket, is reputed to be the final resting place of a gypsy boy who hanged himself one day after losing two stallions he had been entrusted with. The spot has produced colourful flowers all year round ever since and legend has it that the colour of the Derby winner is indicated at sunrise on Derby day by the colour of the flowers on the grave. If dark flowers bloom, a dark horse will win - if light flowers, a light coloured horse.

During the Battle of Waterloo, the Duke of Wellington rode a horse called Copenhagen. After surviving the rigours of war and Waterloo, Copenhagen began a racing career which saw him placed twice in a dozen races and win at Huntingdon. Some time after his racing days were over Copenhagen's name was expunged from the stud book when his dam was proved to be only a half-bred hunting mare. Ironically, Copenhagen was a grandson of the great Eclipse, and the Iron Duke was reportedly not best pleased at this snub to his equine war comrade - someone reportedly remarked to the Duke that it was a pity Copenhagen was not thoroughbred, whereupon he replied, 'Perhaps not down in black and white - but so much more thoroughly bred than most of the men I know.'

A simple stone heads the grave of a horse buried at Roe Hall, Kent. Inscribed upon it are the words 'The Great Dunsterly Bleeder. He Bled To Death.' In a book published in the early 1950s, *World Of Horses*, James Reynolds recounts the bizarre tale of The Dunsterly Bleeder which, Reynolds says, 'Was as strange a case of doomed horseflesh as appears anywhere at any time. Actually, the horse was called Dunsterly Pride by his owner, Squire Hannott of the Grange, Market Harborough. Soon after this horse reached the age of two he began to ooze a dark purplish blood, usually from pores in the region of his hip bones or withers. No one ever knew what brought on this startling condition; no cuts or bruises were responsible. Some old ones said, of course, that the animal was bewitched; he was the devil's steed, of a surety and these bloody patches were the marks of the fiend's hoofs after nocturnal gallops.

'Nothing seemed to stop the bleeding and by now the stallion was known far and wide as the Dunsterly Bleeder. Put to stud he sired big, husky, rather nervous colts. One, Madagascar, won and never showed any ill effects inherited from his bleeding sire. Another, Belfone, won at Newmarket. At the age of eight the Dunsterly Bleeder began to go rapidly downhill. After a terrific bout of bleeding from the mouth when great gouts of dark, black-purple blood pelted down his forelegs it was agreed to destroy the suffering horse.'

The Duke of Westminster held a garden party in 1887, Queen Victoria's Golden Jubilee Year. It was held at Grosvenor House and all the top members of society plus a number of members of various Royal households were present. However, the Guest of Honour was none of these - he travelled to the affair by train from Kingsclere to Waterloo before walking to the Duke's residence where he proceeded to dine in an elegant manner on sugar and flowers - he was the Duke's Derby winner, Ormonde.

A son of the famous Eclipse, Pot-8-os acquired his name when a stable lad told to write the name Potato above the horse's box inscribed Potoooooooo there instead.

Athasi, whose son Trigo won the 1929 Derby, was one of the few racehorses to have been arrested and put in prison. It happened in Ireland when she was being taken to Mr Barnett, by whom she had been purchased. The groom escorting her was arrested for being 'drunk in charge of a mare' and the pair were locked up.

Minoru, the 1909 Derby winner, was later exported to Russia where, so it is alleged, he was seized by the Bolsheviks during the revolution and executed for being an aristocrat.

When Hodge got the bird it was a good sign – for the horse's owner Kay Spence had trained the stable-pet crow to scream 'Come on Hodge' during races. Unfortunately, she couldn't bring the crow to the 1914 Kentucky Derby and Hodge could only finish runner-up to Old Rosebud.

Princely Review became the first yearling to be sold for over 100,000 guineas at public auction in Britain when he went for 117,000 guineas in 1971.

Ghadeer (625,000 guineas) became the first to top the half a million mark in 1979 before Hero Worship went for 1,550,000 guineas in 1983 and Authaal set a new record at 3,100,000 guineas in 1984.

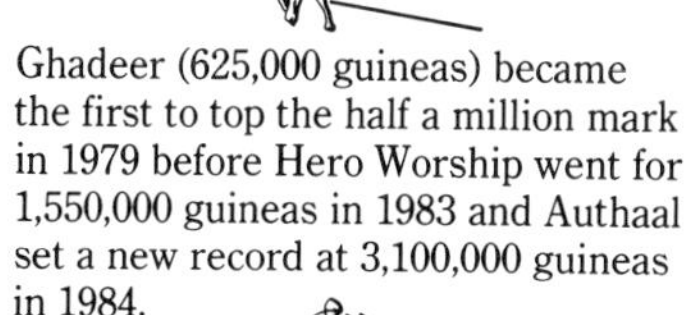

A huge price doesn't necessarily mean success on the racecourse, though, as Sheikh Mohammed Al-Maktoum found out to his cost when he paid $10.2 million for Snaafi Dancer in 1982. The horse was retired in 1985 – without ever setting foot on a racecourse. The only winner in this particular affair was Robert Sangster – who was outbid by the Sheikh for Snaafi Dancer at the Kentucky Keeneland Sales.

Oureone could well be regarded as the least successful racehorse ever. Between December 1976 and November 1983 in Sydney, Australia, the mare raced 124 times, without ever winning.

The eight-year-old Chaplins Club produced a record-breaking run of form over an extraordinary 19 days in 1988, when between July 16 and August 3 he won seven races at six different courses. He started his sequence at Ripon (5–1) ridden by Kevin Darley, who partnered him in all his wins except for the next one, at Ayr on July 18 (6–1). Number three was at Hamilton on July 20 (4-1) before he went to Redcar on July 26 to win at odds of 5–2; Doncaster the next day (11–4), back to Ayr on August 2 to win at 7–4, completing the run the next day at Pontefract, again at odds against, 11–4. Nor was Chaplins Club finished for the season – on September 30 he won again at Haydock, and he did the same thing the very next day. Trainer of Chaplins Club was David Chapman – for whom 1988 was a particularly memorable season as another of his horses, Glencroft, also won nine races.

The name of the 2000 Guineas winner in 1812 was Cwrw.

Red Rum received Official Freedom

to Paddle, Walk or Trot on the beach at Southport, where he was trained, in 1978.

At the height of his fame Red Rum's manure fetched 80p per bag.

Incitatus, a racehorse belonging to Roman Emperor Caligula, was made a citizen of Rome and a Senator by his bizarre owner.

Novice hurdler Red Rascal, who made his debut at Leicester in January 1989, could never be called chicken - a large number of them used to roost on a beam above his box at East Garston, until Red Rascal began to pick them up with his teeth and shake them. 'By the time we realised what was going on he had killed 16 chickens,' recalled owner Nigel Dunger, 'and a guinea fowl. We caught him with a cat once, but that got away.'

The Melbourne syndicate looking for an appropriate name for their filly out of Courtmarsh delved into cricket's folklore to come up with Bowled Lillee!

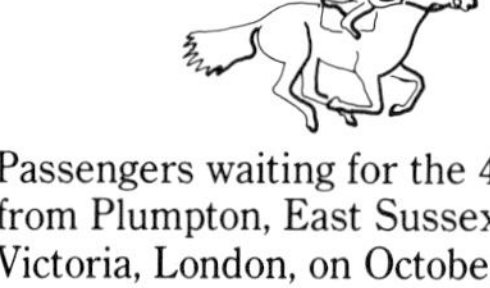

Passengers waiting for the 4.31 train from Plumpton, East Sussex, to Victoria, London, on October 26 1988, were surprised when they were joined on the platform by a racehorse and jockey. Five-year-old mare Our Sedalia and jockey Dale McKeown should have been under orders for the 4.15 at the adjacent Plumpton racecourse but the horse bolted on the way to the start, crashed through two sets of rails and mounted the platform - without even buying a platform ticket. Jockey McKeown managed to pull the mare up before she ended up on the live rail. The pair returned to the course for the race, but pulled up.

Before the advent of motors and air travel horses had it really rough when they had to be transported to meetings. A horse called Cleopatra proves the point - she won the last race at New Zealand's Takapuna meeting and was then put on a harbour ferry to catch a steamer heading for Thames - where it arrived at 1 am. Cleopatra was then walked fifty kilometres to Waihi for an afternoon race which, incredibly, she won.

The bride wore aqua and white, the groom a smile - and the best man had four legs and three tails. When Terry Lee Griffith and Kathleen Boutin, both of Wilmington, Delaware, tied the matrimonial knot in the walking ring at Delaware Park Race Track on Saturday 4 June 1988, there standing as the groom's best man was a racehorse named The Maltese Cat. The 'best man', of course, sported a tuxedo with two tails plus one of his own. Griffith, a 44-year-old trainer based at Delaware Park, has sixteen horses under his care. But 'The Cat' - as he is affectionately called - has a special place in Griffith's heart. In 1983, with his last $1250 and near bankruptcy, Griffith made a four horse purchase which included The Maltese Cat. The Maltese Cat, a six-year-old bay horse, was the best of the lot, going on to win over $40,000 for his trainer, and thereby erasing Griffith's debts. 'I like this horse a lot,' said Griffith. 'Actually, I think I love him.' Following the ceremony, the newlyweds took a ceremonial carriage ride around the race course. They, and their 300 guests, took in a day at the races.

GRAND NATIONAL

Lancet was poised to win the 1836 version of the National when a mounted spectator galloped into him, unseating his rider Alan McDonough.

Boxer Johnny Broome turned jockey to ride Eagle in the 1848 race, but the result was the same. He was knocked out when the horse fell.

Having jumped the last fence in second place in 1849, The Knight Of Gwynne's jockey, Captain D'Arcy, resorted to bribery to try and win. He offered Peter Simple's rider, T Cunningham, amounts starting at £1000 and rising to £4000 for him to 'take a pull'. Cunningham refused.

The Reverend Edward Drake of Shardloes, hiding behind the pseudonym of 'Mr Ekard', finished sixth on Bridegroom in 1860.

In 1868 the favourite, Chimney Sweep, was put down after running into a boulder marking the course, before a fence had been jumped.

Told on the morning of the 1862 race that his sister had died, James Wynne nonetheless went out to ride O'Connell. The horse fell and another horse, Playman, fell on to Wynne, whose internal injuries killed him.

Having unseated his rider, Inkerman managed to leave the course during the 1863 race and wasn't discovered until late that night, in a field several miles away.

Sisters Emblem and Emblematic won the race in 1863 and '64, both ridden by George Stevens who named his home Emblem Cottage. Arbury was second in both races.

1884 winner Voluptuary was sold to actor Leonard Boyne, who put the horse on the stage at the Drury Lane Theatre in 'The Prodigal Daughter'. Each night during the play, the pair would leap a water jump.

Two pounds of butter won the 1901 National for Grudon - the race was run in a blizzard and the course was covered in snow but owner-trainer Bernard Bletsoe bought the butter from a local dairy and rubbed it into Grudon's hooves to prevent the snow balling there.

Becher's Brook gained its name when Captain Becher, riding Conrad, was deposited into the brook immediately after the jump during the running of what some claim to be the first National in 1839.

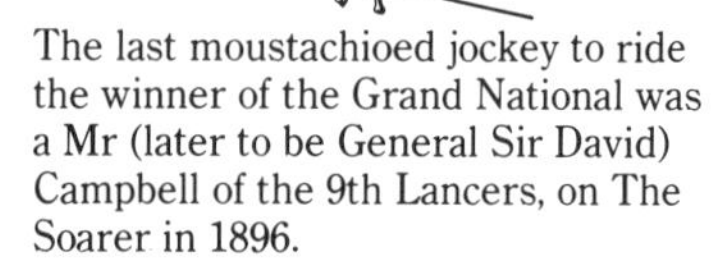

The last moustachioed jockey to ride the winner of the Grand National was a Mr (later to be General Sir David) Campbell of the 9th Lancers, on The Soarer in 1896.

Legend has it that 1904 Grand National winner Moifaa, from New Zealand, was shipwrecked off the coast of Ireland en route to England from the Antipodes, but managed to struggle ashore where local fishermen found him.

So confident were connections of Kirkland before the 1905 National that they paid jockey Frank Mason

'. . . and there goes Captain Becher!'

£300 not to ride in any races for two weeks before the 'big 'un', to avoid the danger of injury. The horse won by three lengths.

1908 winner Rubio was restored to health after injury by pulling the Prospect Arms Hotel of Towcester bus to and from the station every day.

Glenside, the 1911 winner, had only one eye.

All White was moving up to challenge the leaders in 1919 when spectators were amazed to see the horse slow to a walk as his jockey, Frenchman T Williams, was violently sick - the result of a sea-food dish he'd consumed just before the 'off'. The pair continued and finished fifth.

Having remounted on no less than three occasions to finish in fourth place on Turkey Buzzard in 1921, jockey Captain Geoffrey Bennet returned to the paddock expecting the congratulations of owner Mrs M Hollins. Far from congratulating him, Mrs Hollins, outraged at the suffering she felt Bennet had inflicted on the horse, chased him around the paddock aiming blows at him with her umbrella.

Bennet, who won the 1923 race on Sergeant Murphy, was killed on December 27 of that year when he fell on Ardeen at Wolverhampton and was kicked in the head. He never regained consciousness and died 17 days later. Following this accident, crash helmets became compulsory.

Rejected as being of no account and put to work as a plough horse in Donegal, Master Robert was bought for £50, and went on to win the 1924 National.

Only two of the 42 starters completed the course in 1928 when 100-1 shot Tipperary Tim beat 33-1 chance Billy Barton.

The Grand National was won by two furlongs in 1935 - or, more accurately, two Furlongs. Major Noel Furlong was the owner and trainer and son Frank the rider of Reynoldstown.

Amateur jockey Major W H Skrine was so desperate to ride his horse Martin M in the 1947 National that he had an operation to shorten one of his legs to match the other which had been injured during the War. The Major and Martin M parted company once during the race but he remounted to finish 12th. The race, run in a heavy mist, was won by 100-1 shot Caughoo, whose jockey Eddie Dempsey was, some years later, involved in a punch-up with the jockey of the runner-up Lough Conn when that worthy, Daniel McCann, accused Dempsey of having taken a short cut in the fog! The case ended up in court but was quickly dismissed.

Mr What, the 1958 winner, never won again in 33 attempts.

There has never been, and almost certainly never will be, another jockey like the Duque de Albuquerque.

The Duque saw a film about the Grand National in the 1920s, fell in love with the race and vowed to win it. He never did, but it wasn't through lack of trying. In his 34th year, 1952, the Duque achieved the first part of his ambition by competing in the National. He rode his own horse, Brown Jack III, and the pair hit the deck at the 6th, the Duque ending up in hospital with a cracked vertebra.

He was back eleven years later, riding Jonjo. They got as far as the 21st where they fell, without much damage to either party. Attempt No. 3 came in 1965 when he bought and rode Groomsman, and down they came at the 9th. Off went the Duque to hospital with a broken leg, the 22nd time he had broken or fractured part of his body.

L'Empereur carried the Duque in 1966 and they did well to reach the 26th fence before the horse decided he'd done enough and pulled up. Seven years passed, during which time the Duque went elsewhere to get injured, managing ten more fractures. In 1973 he was back for a fifth attempt, this time riding the seven-year-old Nereo; they were the youngest horse and the oldest jockey. But for a leather which broke, causing them to pull up, they might well have got round.

Some weeks before the 1974 National the Duque had an accident in Seville which necessitated the insertion of 16 screws in his leg and they were only removed a fortnight before the big race. A week before the race he broke his collar bone. But, at the age of 55, he completed the course at the sixth attempt, finishing eighth on Nereo in the process. Flushed with success the Duque plotted his 1975 bid for glory, only to break a leg a week before the race. But even then he was willing to take a chance, until trainer Fred Winter pointed out that it might be somewhat unfair on Nereo.

April 3, 1976 – the Duque lined up for his seventh ride in the National. Racing up with the leaders he and Nereo capsized at the 13th – 'I have been superstitious of that number all my life,' said the Duque – and once again he took up residence in hospital. He'd been trampled on after the fall and didn't regain consciousness for over two days, when he discovered that he had seven broken ribs, broken vertebrae, a broken wrist, a fractured right thigh bone . . . oh yes, and severe concussion.

The end of the line? Well, everybody thought so except the gallant Duque who said, 'I still want to return and complete the course on a Spanish horse.' At this point the Jockey Club stepped in, refused the Duque permission to ride over fences and also introduced a rule requiring amateur riders of over fifty to undergo a stringent medical examination. The Duque's reaction? 'I was very sad. I trained hard for the 1977 National and considered myself fitter than I had been for years. Then they banned me.'

Three Russian horses were sent over for the race in 1961. Epigraf was injured and couldn't race, Reljef fell at the first brook, and Grifel pulled up, having been remounted after falling at Becher's.

A jockey fighting cancer and a horse written off after breaking down with leg trouble proved the most emotional winners ever of the National when Bob Champion and Aldaniti stormed home in 1981.

48-year-old Dick Saunders was the oldest jockey to win the National when Grittar triumphed in 1982.

Headmaster Peter Roger holds the record time for completing the Grand National course without the aid of a horse. In 1983 he went round in 40 minutes to raise £6000 for the St Michael's Junior School in Kirkby.

Grand National winner Corbiere was given a change of scenery, by competing in show jumping events.

The day before the 1986 Grand National was run, Steve Smith Eccles, who was due to partner the fancied Classified, was taking a nap in the back seat of his Mercedes when he suddenly awoke to find the car in motion – it had been stolen with him in it! 'The thief was as shocked as I was when he saw me bob up; he panicked and eventually pulled into the hard shoulder, got out and bolted.' Smith Eccles was none the worse for his experience – riding Classified into third place.

The 1938 winner Battleship was ridden by the youngest winning jockey, 17-year-old Bruce Hobbs, and owned by Marion du Pont Scott, wife of Hollywood cowboy film star Randolph.

In 1956 the Queen Mother's Devon Loch, ridden by future best-selling author, Dick Francis, was well clear with under fifty yards to run when he inexplicably collapsed, allowing E S B to win.

Owen's Sedge, owned by actor Gregory Peck, finished seventh in 1963. Peck tried again in 1967 with Different Class – but it was no such thing, the 100–8 chance was brought down. In 1968 he did somewhat better, finishing third, with 68-year-old American grandfather Tim Durant remounting to finish 15th on Highlandie.

Shortly before the start of the 1964 race, a plane crashed near the Canal Turn, killing all of its five occupants, among them television personality Nancy Spain who was flying up as a guest of Aintree owner Mrs Topham.

Holiday camp king Fred Pontin owned the 1971 winner Specify.

Norwegian Flag, owned by singer Dorothy Squires, was 10th in 1974 behind Red Rum, winning for the second successive year.

'Teazy Weazy' hairdresser P B Raymond won with Ayala in 1963 and Rag Trade in 1976.

Liverpool and England soccer star Emlyn Hughes couldn't watch his Wayward Scot run in the 1979 National because he was playing in the FA Cup Semi Final - but he didn't miss much, his horse fell at the 1st.

Television presenter Desmond Lynam leased Another Duke to run in his colours in 1986 and there was much speculation about how he would interview himself as the winning owner should the horse prevail. It wasn't a problem - the horse, a 200-1 chance, fell.

Professional gambler Alex Bird nearly pulled off his biggest ever coup when his own horse, Tudor Line, finished second, beaten by a neck in the 1954 Grand National. He stood to win half a million.

Middlesbrough businessman Alf Duffield bet £20,000 to win £750,000 on his horse Tacroy in the 1984 Grand National. The horse was unplaced. In 1985 he backed it again, to win £630,000. Tacroy pulled up, but Duffield had also staked £500 each way on Last Suspect at 66-1 and collected £41,250.

Terry Ramsden, one-time owner of Walsall FC, staked over £100,000 on his horse Mr Snugfit to win the 1986 National. He got his money back when the horse finished fourth. He'd have won over a million had the horse won.

WHAT DID THEY DO IN THE WAR?

When the Second World War broke out the owners of the Beech House Stud in Newmarket immediately set about constructing three air raid shelters - one for proprietor Martin Benson, one for his staff and one for resident stallion, Nearco.

A prisoner of war camp, a hay dispersal centre, a tank testing ground, a munitions depot and a troop camp - these were amongst the uses to which Newbury racecourse was put during the First World War. It was in demand again during the second war when the US Armed Forces took it over as a supply depot, burying the turf under thirty five miles of railway lines and concrete roads. After extensive repair work, the course was able to reopen for racing in April 1949.

Champion jockey Sir Gordon Richards was turned down when he tried to join the RAF and the Army at the outbreak of the Second World War, because of a history of tuberculosis in his medical records.

New Zealand jockey Pat Spratt thought he'd come up with a great excuse to avoid being called up for the forces during the Second World War. He would get too heavy and be unable to continue his career, he pleaded to the Christchurch Committee who had to make a decision. They obviously weren't racing men - Spratt lost.

Racehorses were rationed to 8lbs of oats per day.

Less than a quarter of the 11,000 horses which had been in training prior to the outbreak of war were still in training at the end.

Jockey Tommy Hawcroft won the 'Palestine Donkey Grand National' whilst serving there in the Royal Veterinary Corps.

Epsom racecourse gave up its iron railings for scrap to help the War effort.

Forestation's prize money from the Champion Hurdle in 1942 was donated by owner Victor Smyth to the Red Cross Fund.

Nearly 2000 acres of Jockey Club land in Newmarket was requisitioned for military purposes, leaving less than 500 for racing and training.

The saddle in which Sam Wragg rode Pont L'Eveque to win the 1940 Derby was auctioned and the proceeds donated to the Red Cross Fund.

Only 14 days' racing took place between the outbreak of war in September 1939 and the end of that year.

The 1939 St Leger was abandoned.

Prize money was badly affected – one meeting at Wetherby offered a maximum prize of £58. The Grand National in 1940 was worth just £4150 to the winner, compared with £7384 in 1939.

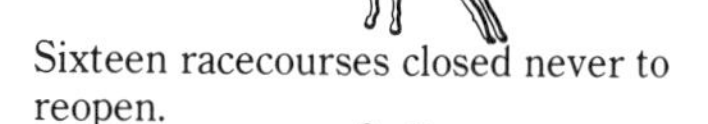

Sixteen racecourses closed never to reopen.

Aintree was requisitioned so the 1940 National was the last of the War. The Derby and Oaks were switched to Newmarket.

Despite strong criticism in some quarters that racing was allowed to continue, King George VI attended

the 1942 Derby and Oaks – his Sun Chariot won the Oaks at 4–1. She had already won the 1000 Guineas, and his Big Game had won the 2000.

Racing writer Roger Mortimer, a prisoner of war, tuned in on the camp's secret wireless to the broadcast of the 1944 Derby – blowing a valve in the set in the process. To avoid the displeasure of fellow prisoners he had to trade a large number of cigarettes for a new valve from a 'tame' guard.

When King Penguin won a race over the sticks at Ludlow in October 1946, it was the first winner for the partnership between jockey Dick Black and trainer John de Moraville, who had met and formed their partnership in a German prisoner of war camp. They went on to turn out many more winners.

Trainer Marcus Marsh, who sent out Windsor Lad to win the Derby and St Leger in 1934, enlisted in the RAF at the start of the War and served as a rear gunner in bomber command. He was shot down over Holland in 1941 and as a prisoner of war was involved in the famous 'Wooden Horse' escape.

Four jockeys who had ridden Grand National winners died during the Second World War hostilities. They were Frank Furlong (Reynoldstown, 1935) of Fleet Air Arm; Bobby Everett (Gregalach, 1929) of the Royal Navy; Mervyn Jones (Bogskar, 1940) of the RAF and Tommy

Cullinan (Shaun Goilin, 1930), serving with an anti-aircraft unit.

Then a jockey, later a trainer, Bill Marshall was mentioned in despatches and served as a fighter pilot, winning the DFC, during the War.

Frank Wise lost a leg and the tops of three fingers during the First World War – but that didn't stop him riding Alike to victory in the 1929 Irish Grand National.

Australian owner Charlie Butler was delighted when his Valiant Gamble won the 120,000 dollar Hiskens Chase at Moonee Valley in 1989 – after all, few dead people own such a good winner. Butler was officially declared 'dead' after a battle on the Owen Stanley Range in New Guinea in 1942, and his name even appears on the Roll of Honour at the Melbourne Cricket Club. However Butler, shot several times in the face, survived the incident and returned to full health to the astonishment of friends who thought he was dead and buried.

German Derby winner Alchimist was the victim of a bizarre incident during the war. The horse was at Gradiz, the German National Stud, in 1945 when Russian troops launched their invasion. The Stud's grooms fled, leaving Alchimist behind. When they returned for the valuable stallion they discovered that the starving troops had eaten him, enjoying in the process perhaps the most expensive meal ever consumed.

There was a shortage of competent racing staff during the War. At one stage Fred Wood, who had been a

jockey during the reign of Queen Victoria, was doing riding work, and Jack Jarvis re-employed a stable lad who had been working for him as long ago as the turn of the century. Captain Percy Whitaker, who rode in the 1906 National, was riding out too.

Popular owner Lord Glanely, whose nickname was Old Guts and Gaiters, was killed during an air-raid. Grand Parade had won the 1919 Derby for him.

All over Germany, it would seem, inmates were clustered around secret wireless sets in the prisoner of war camps straining their ears to listen to the BBC commentary on the 1944 Derby. The result brought no joy to the racing mad captives, though, the winner was a 28–1 outsider Ocean Swell and one camp bookie, James Marsham who went on to become a stewards' secretary, cleaned up.

Racing at Hong Kong's Happy Valley continued under Japanese occupation during the war, but some unusual runners had to be found to make up the numbers. One horse called Wor Ngau (appropriately, The Snail) was only 3ft 7ins tall and another, Kau Loong, had been pulling a bus. Kau Loong's chances were considered so remote that he was given a 600 metre start and a weight of just 124lbs. However punters reckoned without his relief at having no bus to pull – he won easily!

By the end of the occupation, horses were in such short supply in Hong Kong that programmes were supplemented by races for wooden horses made of three-ply, 15½ in long and 8½ in high. They 'galloped' down a contraption of wires in front of the grandstand and winners were penalised by having weights removed so they would slide down the wires more slowly!

TURF TRAINERS

TECHNIQUES

One lesser known method of encouraging horses to run faster is to implant magnets in their hooves. They are particularly useful, apparently, to help nurse injured horses back to full health. Dr Aarre Salo, a scientist in Australia, claims, 'They are placed in the wall of the hoof and act as a virtual blood pump. This accelerates the healing process.' The tiny magnets are glued into place on either side of the hoof and top

trainer Bart Cummings says, 'There is every reason why it should work. Once you improve the blood flow through a horse's legs, he can be worked stronger.'

The 4th Duke of Portland, whose Tiresias won the 1819 Derby, had rather unconventional ideas about training his horses. He felt that they should always be prepared for any unexpected shock or noise which might affect them at the racecourse, so he would ride them past a drum and fife band and bring in men from his Newmarket estate to shout and wave flags at the horses. He would also explode squibs suddenly in the horses' stables, as part of the unorthodox treatment.

Space is at such a premium in Hong Kong that many horses carry out their morning exercise walks on the tops of skyscrapers.

Here's a tip to be 'born' in mind. Veterinary science proves that fillies who have just gone into foal usually improve their form by the equivalent of a few pounds as a result of the pregnancy, which releases hormones and cortisones into their system.

The story is told of Ilsely trainer Harry Barnes who, it is said, once took time off from his horses to train pigs to jump hurdles! Many years ago, revealed the 1963 Sporting News Annual, Barnes trained for a medical man called Dr Hutton, who was so proud of his trainer that he struck a wager with two wealthy young gentlemen, Walter Long of Christ Church College, Oxford and Lamont Rose of Brasenose, that Barnes could train pigs to jump hurdles. The bet was made for £1000, so Barnes went to work, laying out a course and putting up eight flights of hurdles, each two feet six inches high. The great day arrived and the eight pigs were ready to jump to it. Just to stimulate their interest and keep their minds on business, Barnes had kept them without food all day. The starter got them all into a line and Harry Barnes set off over the centre flight of hurdles with a food pail in his hand – and all the pigs went steaming off after the smell. At the same time stable lads stationed at the end of the track began to bang and rattle food pails. With dinner in sight, those porkers leaped and amid uproarious cheering, all eight got round and the wager was won.

ACHIEVEMENTS

Saddling the winner of the Cheltenham Gold Cup is generally reckoned to be the pinnacle of a trainer's career, but when Arthur Stephenson's The Thinker won the great race in 1987, the trainer was so blase about the event that he watched it on TV from Hexham racecourse.

Trainer Fulke Walwyn and owner Dorothy Paget were a little disappointed when Loyal Monarch was beaten by half a length in the last race at Folkestone in September 1948, but their disappointment was slightly alleviated by the fact that they had already been responsible for five earlier winners on the card – Legal Joy, Langis Son, Jack Tatters, Endless and Loyal King.

New Zealand trainer Arthur Didham sent out his first winner on Boxing Day 1929, and didn't stop saddling winners until 58 years later.

When Orby won the 1907 Derby his trainer, Colonel Frederick McCabe, who had been medical officer to the South Irish Horse regiment, sent a telegram to the commanding officer, saying 'Medical Officer authorises the issue of champagne to all ranks.' The issue duly took place and celebrations were memorable.

Sam Darling, who trained seven Classic winners, was obsessively neat and tidy, literally to the day he died in 1921. On the day of his funeral the streets of the village of Beckhampton, where he trained, were swept clean and sanded, in accordance with his will. His coffin was carried by farm carts newly-painted in colours he had specified.

Captain Sir Cecil Boyd-Rochfort, born in Ireland in 1887 and top trainer five times as well as training thirteen Classic winners, was knighted for his services to racing in 1968.

Trainer Jack Jarvis was knighted for his services to racing in 1967.

The only known instance of a trainer receiving a medal for 'integrity' took place in 1873 when James Binnie was presented with a specially struck silver medal by the executive of

Scotland's Hawick racecourse. The inscription on the medal reads, 'Presented to James Binnie by the Stewards and committee for his long attendance and integrity in running horses at Hawick.'

Neville Crump, who trained three Grand National winners, recalled the time he was stopped going into the car park at Aintree and asked by the gateman who he was. 'Who the hell do you think I am? I'm Neville Crump, I've trained three Grand National winners here.'

'Oh yeah!' said the gateman. 'That's what the last bloke who came in here with his car said to me.'

The last man through the car park, unbeknown to Crump (and the gateman!), was Fred Rimell, who had also trained three National winners . . .

Trainer Peter Purcell Gilpin was so keen to ensure that news of the secret trial he had given his 1906 Derby hope Spearmint didn't leak out and cause the horse's odds to drop, that he literally locked the jockeys who had taken part in the trial into the house in which they were dining before setting off to back the horse at the longest possible odds. Gilpin was able to back Spearmint at 20–1 and the horse went on to win the Derby at 6–1.

Trainers are not generally known for their fashion sense but Rod Simpson is different and flamboyant – and unapologetic. He told the Sporting Life, 'I wear leather suits a lot. I get stick from members of the Jockey Club and local stewards because they look at you as if to say, "I don't think he should be allowed in here wearing that". I don't think they should be allowed anywhere looking like they do.' Simpson is also one of the few trainers who would confess that his favourite music is heavy metal.

In 1801 Mr Cox, trainer for leading Turf figure Sir Charles Bunbury, gave a tip for a horse with his dying breath. His last words, uttered to a clergyman were, 'Depend upon it, that Eleanor is one hell of a mare.' A few weeks later she went on to win the Derby and the Oaks.

Great trainer Mathew Dawson, responsible for 28 Classic winners, died of politeness. In 1898, at the age of 78, he was visited by the Prince of Wales, who engaged him in conversation. Dawson was standing in a draught but was too polite to turn his back and close the offending window. As a result he caught a chill and died.

Despite having trained many big race winners, including three of the Grand National, Captain Tim Forster is widely regarded as being the game's biggest pessimist. He readily admits that his advice to Charlie Fenwick immediately before he rode the 1980 winner Ben Nevis in the National was 'Keep remounting'. And when he was discussing Last Suspect's chances with connections, prior to the horse's long-odds triumph, he advised them to 'meet back at the weighing room after we've caught him'. Unmarried, perhaps it is not hard to see why when the Captain has been quoted as saying, 'The perfect wife would be a great help – but the imperfect wife might be a grave nuisance.' In his study he keeps a number of postcards, sporting such encouraging phrases as 'The situation is hopeless and getting worse' and 'Yesterday was a dead loss, today is even worse, tomorrow is cancelled.' When announcing that his chaser Pegwell Bay was to be aimed for the 1989 Gold Cup, Forster added, 'In theory he has no chance' but justified the decision to try anyway by saying, 'I might be dead next year, the owner might be dead next year, and the horse might be dead next year.'

When jockey Mornington Cannon rode his first winner in 1887 he was just 13. Trainer Charles Morton congratulated him and gave him a sovereign, telling him to buy sweets with it. Mornington got his name as he was born on the very day that his father Thomas rode a horse of that name to victory at Bath.

Top trainer Jem Godding, who sent out Classic winners in 1862 and '63, lost himself all the horses in his care owned by the wealthy but eccentric Earl of Glasgow when he tried to tell that worthy a small joke. The Earl was visiting the stables and chanced upon a useful horse called Volunteer. 'The owner has never seen this colt although he only lives a few miles from here,' Godding told the Earl, who was most indignant - until Godding told him that the owner was blind! Lord Glasgow chased Godding all around his yard and promptly had all his horses removed from there.

Trainer Charles Morton was not always pleased with the choice of

horses made by his leading owner Robert Sievier, a legendary gambler, and when Sievier sent him a horse called Lavengro in 1900, an enormous ugly colt, Morton sent him in return a telegram saying, 'Lavengro arrived. This is not a brewery.' However, Sievier had the last laugh when Lavengro won some good races.

Trainer Sir Mark Prescott is not usually a bad loser, but when he failed to retain a horse which had just won a selling race for him at the subsequent auction, he snatched the bridle off of the horse, 'then stomped home leaving the new, proud owner with his arms around the horse's neck shrieking for a bridle.' Sir Mark told the *Sporting Life*, 'This fit of pique resulted in a new rule that it was the duty of the trainer of the animal at the time it won to take the horse back to the racecourse stables, whatever the result of the auction - this probably represents my only long term footprint in turf history.'

At the beginning of the 20th century with doping of horses a real problem, trainer George Lambton deliberately doped five of his own horses - who, despite having no previous form, then won four races and finished second in the other - in order to draw attention to the problem.

THE DERBY

The Derby is the most important Flat race in England, perhaps the world - but it could easily have been known as the Bunbury, for in 1781 Lord Derby and Sir Charles Bunbury tossed a coin for the right to have a new race named after them and the noble Lord won.

Diomed, the 6-4 favourite won the first running of the Derby in 1781. It was owned by . . . Sir Charles Bunbury.

Sir John Lade owned Crop, the runner up in the 1782 Derby. But his biggest claim to fame was that he was the first man to wear long trousers in public.

Lord George Bentinck proposed that Parliament should take the day off in order to be able to attend the 1848 Derby. The motion was duly carried and Bentinck was able to watch Surplice, a horse he had once owned, win the race. The Derby Day adjournment then became an annual event for the next forty years and was still moved into the early 20th century even though the political climate had changed by then and the motion was being regularly defeated.

The 1791 winner, Eager, subsequently became the only Derby winner to run in a selling race.

The 1797 winner had no name. He was known merely as the Duke of Bedford's brown colt by Fidget out of a sister of Pharamond.

Eleanor became the first of six fillies to win the race, in 1801.

Riding the 1808 Derby winner Pan cost jockey Frank Collinson his life – on his way to Epsom he slept in a damp bed at an inn, contracting the disease which killed him three years later.

Smolensko, the first black horse to win the Derby (1813) was also the first horse to complete the 2000 Guineas–Derby double.

Raphael started 7–2 favourite for the 1815 Derby but was beaten into second place by Whisker. The crowd was not best pleased and Raphael's jockey, J Jackson was dragged from the horse and attacked. He survived.

Sam Chifney became the first jockey to ride a Derby winner named after himself when Sam won in 1818.

Only one horse has ever won the Derby on his own birthday – Sailor on May 18, 1820.

Gustavus, in 1821, was the first grey Derby winner.

In 1827 one William Dorling produced the first Derby race-card entirely unofficially.

The 1837 Derby plays a prominent part in Benjamin Disraeli's novel, *Sybil*.

Racegoers rioted when places on the first-ever 'Derby Special' trains from Nine Elms station ran out in 1838.

In 1841 the 29 Derby runners came under orders at 2.30 - and started at 4pm.

In 1846 Sir Tatton Sykes finished second to Pyrrhus The First. But all contemporary reports agree that Sir Tatton Sykes would surely have won, had his jockey Bill Scott not been as drunk as a lord.

The tail and one of the legs of the 1850 Derby and St Leger winner Voltigeur are on display at York's racing museum.

200–1 outsider Black Tommy was so little fancied for the 1857 Derby that one bookie laid the owner, Mr Drinkald a bet of £10,000 to a suit against the horse winning - it finished second to Blink Bonny.

Only one man ever both rode a Derby winner and started the race. Henry Custance won on Thormanby in 1860 and acted as starter in 1885.

Caractacus beat 33 rivals in 1862 - the largest field.

Gladiateur was the first French winner in 1865 and with the English not noted for their generosity in defeat at this time, the French newspaper *Le Petit Journal* reported that the horse's connections had hired six hundred boxers to protect them and the horse.

The current Derby course was first used in 1872.

In 1873, Doncaster came to Epsom - and won the Derby at odds of 45–1, ridden by Fred Webb.

Solicitor W S Cartwright was so confident that his 9–1 shot George Frederick would win the 1874 Derby that he wrote out 30 victory telegrams to send to friends in advance. He won by 2 lengths.

The great Fred Archer won the 1880 Derby - riding with one arm! The other one had been savaged by a horse some weeks earlier and was bound to a piece of iron to enable him to ride Bend Or, on whom he duly won.

Dealings on Wall Street were suspended on Wednesday June 1, 1881, when the news came in that Iroquois had become the first American winner of the Derby.

Before the start of the 1883 Derby a fire broke out on the Epsom Downs - and many coincidence backers cleaned up as St Blaise won the big race at odds of 11-2. 26 years later the horse was burnt to death in a fire at the Nursery Stud in America.

The skeleton of 1886 Derby winner Ormonde can be seen at the Natural History Museum in London.

Ladas, the 1894 winner completed the two boyhood ambitions of the fifth Earl of Rosebery: to own a Derby winner and to become Prime Minister, which he had done just a few weeks earlier.

Albert Edward, Prince of Wales, later to become King Edward VII was the owner of 1896 winner Persimmon. He won again in 1909 with Minoru.

The 1913 running was an eventful affair - suffragette Emily Davison darted on to the course at Tattenham Corner and attempted to grab the reins of the King's colt Anmer. Horse and jockey fell but were not too badly hurt but Davison fractured her skull and died several days later. The race was won by 6-4 favourite Craganour who was disqualified in favour of 100-1 runner-up Aboyeur. Craganour's owner, C Bower Ismay, was a survivor of the Titanic disaster.

From 1915-1918 the Derby was run at Newmarket as Epsom was requisitioned by the military during the course of the First World War.

Two weeks after winning the 1921 Derby, Humorist died from a tubercular lung condition.

Call Boy's 1927 victory was the first broadcast by the BBC.

The 1932 winner, April the Fifth was trained by former well-known stage actor Tom Walls, famous for his roles in West End farces.

1934 also-ran Bondsman was used as a hack by General Eisenhower during the war.

Bois Roussel won the first televised Derby in 1938.

The finish of the 1959 Derby was a real family affair, with Harry Carr on Parthia winning from his son-in-law Joe Mercer on Fidalgo.

In 1962 seven horses fell five furlongs from home, including the favourite Hethersett, leaving Larkspur to win what had started as a 26-runner race.

The O'Brien family dominated the 1984 Derby with David O'Brien-trained Secreto winning by a short head from the odds-on El Gran Senor, trained by his father, Vincent.

Pop star Billy Fury's Anselmo was fourth in 1964, behind winner Santa Claus.

Who is the only Egyptian to have trained the winner of the English Derby? Maurice Zilber (Empery 1976).

The slowest Derby winning time recorded is 3min 4secs by Ellington in 1856. The fastest is 2min 34secs by Mahmoud in 1936.

It's not only racegoers who get stuck in Derby Day traffic jams - in 1932 winning horse April the Fifth and his owner-trainer Tom Walls had to make their own way to the course having been stuck in a slow moving line of vehicles. In 1971, the Queen's trainer Ian Balding had to run two miles clad in top hat and tails, to make it to the course in time to see Mill Reef win. And in 1988 jockey Michael Roberts cadged a lift on the back of a motor-bike to make it to Epsom in time to ride.

CELEBRITY RACEGOERS

PUNTERS

Famous *Daily Mail* columnist Nigel Dempster had plenty to gossip about when he pulled off a betting coup with his own horse, My Purple Prose. He persuaded his bookmaker to offer him odds of 200–1 against the horse winning three races during the 1988–89 jump season. Dempster staked £50 and collected £10,000 when the horse won at Chepstow in March 1989 at evens, having first obliged at Chepstow in January at 16–1 and at Towcester at 5–6.

TV comic and impressionist Enn Reitel thought he'd found the way to untold riches as a youngster when he began to follow the tips of clairvoyant Maurice Woodruffe. 'He said the 1965 Lincoln was going to be won by a horse with a man's name, and the paper-round money went on Old Tom, who came in at 22–1. Then he said the National was going to be won by a horse with one white sock who'd come across water. My brother and I looked through the field and decided it had to be Vulcabo at 66–1. We couldn't work out quite where the water came in but we thought maybe he'd have to go on the Mersey Ferry or something to get to Aintree from Findon. I also fancied Jay Trump (from America) and I'll never forget when he walked in after winning seeing just a flash of white above his hind hoof and realising we'd got the wrong one. It took me two weeks to get over that.'

Cockney comedian Dave Cook achieved a feat recognised by the Guinness Book of Records when, in November 1989, he recited the names of the last 43 Derby winners in the correct order in 16 seconds.

According to his show business friend Bill Waddington – Percy Sugden of Coronation Street fame – comedian Sid James had an unusual betting system. Said Waddington, 'For years Sid had a standing bet with his bookie on any horse at odds of 9–1. First time out for one of my horses, I put on a tenner and it came in at 9–1. Now I only go for those odds.'

Cricket legend Sir Gary Sobers backed three horses one day in August, 1968. They all won at odds of 10–1, 20–1 and 4–1, and shortly afterwards, Sir Gary went out to bat against Glamorgan. He celebrated by hitting six sixes in one over.

David Coleman is a keen follower of the racing game. In fact, he was a member of the Royal Commission on Gambling, and he's backed his fair share of winners over the years. 'I always followed the National, and it's always been a lucky race for me. My family like a bob or two on the horses and I've been backing the National winner ever since Royal

Mail won at 100–6 in 1937. I generally back three or four horses and I've nearly always had the winner. I very much wanted Josh Gifford to win on Honey End in 1967 but he was second in that remarkable race to the 100–1 outsider Foinavon; and guess which horse I drew in the BBC sweep? Yes, Foinavon.'

Pop star Steve Harley was a great fan of Derby winner Shergar, and he was so devastated when his equine hero was unexpectedly trounced in the St Leger that he completely forgot he'd won £200 on the winner of the race, Cut Above, 'just in case'.

Music critic and jazz buff Benny Green tells an amusing cautionary gambling tale. 'My great uncle Jack made a comfortable living by placing bets on the course on behalf of owners whose presence at the bookies' stand might have spoiled the odds. One morning he boarded the train at King's Cross bound for Doncaster with £500 to be wagered on the favourite nag of a certain racing peer. On the train he met a well-known jockey who had been sent to replace another who had broken his leg. The horse the jockey was to ride was the same one my great uncle was going to back. He gave half the stake money to the jockey, kept half for himself, disembarked at Peterborough and came home, while the jockey went on to make sure the horse finished a respectable fifth.'

Former Deputy Prime Minister, Viscount Willie Whitelaw, fancied backing the one horse he had ever owned in partnership. 'It's such a long time ago, I can't even remember the animal's name, but our trainer told us to keep our money in our pockets as the horse hadn't any chance at all.' It trotted up at long odds!

Author Graham Greene never forgave himself for not backing 10–1 winner Brighton Rock when he visited Brighton races whilst researching his best selling novel, Brighton Rock.

Sir Alec Douglas Home, former Conservative Prime Minister is a bit of a judge when it comes to backing horses and he has come to a satisfactory arrangement with his brother William, a playwright. Said Sir Alec in the *Sunday Times*, 'He and I are both very keen on racing. He rings me up and asks me for winners. I charge him 10% now, because we had a great coup at Ascot and I said I wouldn't give him another tip unless he gave me 10% of the winnings.'

The then Shadow Minister for Sport, Dennis Howell, surprised colleagues by the vehemence of a 1985 speech about soccer hooligans which he made in the House of Commons. The reason for the aggression shown by Mr Howell was revealed later when he told colleagues that he'd been called in at short notice to make the speech, had had to cancel a day at Cheltenham races and, worst of all, hadn't had time to back the three horses he'd picked out, all of which won.

Magician Paul Daniels failed to pull off a trick for once when he sponsored a race at Redcar, the Paul Daniels Magic Handicap. He entered his own horse, That's Magic, in the race and she finished 15th of the 18 starters.

After telling actor Fred Feast (then playing barman Fred Gee) 'Fred, don't touch me' during a Coronation Street rehearsal, actress Julie Goodyear, alias Bet Lynch, was astonished when Fred told her a horse called Don't Touch was running that afternoon. She risked £1 on the nose and it won at 25–1.

TV personality Henry Kelly revealed how he backed the winner of the 1961 Grand National after a school pal, Jimmy Weldon, dreamt that a grey horse won the race. Sure enough, there was a grey horse entered, Nicolaus Silver, and Kelly and Weldon between them gambled half a crown each way. 'I listened to the race on the wireless and could hardly believe my ears as Nicolaus Silver won. It was a sign from God that racing was a straight and decent pursuit for Catholic boys.' The horse returned 28–1.

In March 1989, Wimbledon soccer club manager Bobby Gould revealed that he had an unusual clause written into his contract - permission to attend Cheltenham races on Gold Cup day. And he proved the wisdom of insisting on that clause when he went to Cheltenham and cleaned up by backing 66–1 shot Observer Corps.

OWNERS

Here's a talented five-a-side soccer team of racehorse owners:
Peter Shilton (goalkeeper) - Between The Sticks
Bryan Robson (midfield) - Taylormade Boy
Mick Channon (striker) - Cathy Jane
Kevin Keegan (striker) - Man On The Run
Francis Lee (striker) - String Player

Soccer star turned trainer, Francis Lee, first owned a horse after a £26 bet he and fellow Derby player Rod Thomas had placed won them £2500 with which they bought Clydebank. 'I remember the first time we really fancied it,' recalls Lee. 'He was running at Chepstow but it was a Saturday and we were playing Wolves at home so we couldn't go. That morning the assistant manager Des Anderson came in and told me and Rod, "I've got some very bad news for you". We thought, "Bloody hell, the horse has broken a leg", but instead he told us the match had been abandoned. We said, "What a shame". But really it was all we could do to stop laughing. We raced down to Chepstow and watched the horse scoot in at 8–1. When he won his next race as well, I thought it was all so easy. I soon found out it was not.'

Midfield player Ian Snodin organised a syndicate of Everton footballers to lease a horse to run in their name for the 1989 season. Called Dan The Man, Mike O'Neill trained the horse near Aintree.

In hospital with a damaged knee, footballer Liam Brady met jump jockey Stan Moore, in with a broken shoulder and cracked pelvis. They got talking, Brady revealed he'd been thinking of buying a racehorse, Moore put him onto trainer Richard

Hannon - with the result that Brady became owner of Only The Lonely.

Bournemouth FC manager, Harry Redknapp, went into ownership in 1989 with Slick Cherry, trained by David Elsworth.

Former England soccer skippers Mick Channon and Kevin Keegan ruined their training programmes when they went into partnership with Man On The Run. Remembers Channon, 'After finally persuading Kevin to come into partnership, I got him to come along to the races. Our horse came last, so we got legless on champagne.' But when another of Channon's horses, Jamesmead, won the 1988 Tote Gold Trophy at Newbury, the former soccer star said that the victory had given him more pleasure than the 300 goals he scored in his career with England, Southampton, Manchester City, Norwich City and Portsmouth.

England goalkeeper Peter Shilton was choked when his unraced two-year-old, Between The Sticks, won first time out at Newmarket in April, 1989 at odds of 33–1. Shilton had arrived at the course too late to back the horse.

Sir Winston Churchill was a keen and lucky owner. The first he owned, Colonist II, won eleven races including The Winston Churchill Stakes at Hurst Park in 1951. Once the horse's racing career was over, however. Churchill refused to send him to stud, saying, 'I don't want to end my days living on the immoral earnings of a horse.'

Sir Winston's racing colours were Pink, Chocolate sleeves and cap.

Former MP Sir Clement Freud is a keen racegoer - and keen on everything else to do with the sport. He has owned several horses including, recently, one which was named after a famous remark by Mrs Thatcher, 'Weareagrandmother'. He once even rode one of his horses, Winter Fair, in a match against Harrods' owner Sir Hugh Fraser, and he claims to have been a punter since the age of ten, once telling the Sunday Express, 'I don't think I've ever had a bet which was so insignificant that it didn't hurt when I lost. It isn't that I would put up huge sums so much as that I would put on a bet that would win me a huge sum.'

Here's an attractive variety show line-up of racehorse owners:
Roger de Courcey (Ventriloquist) - Nookie Bear
Paul Daniels (Magician) - That's Magic
Freddie Starr (Comedian) - Captiva
Dorothy Squires (Singer) - Esban

One of the greatest hoofers of all time, Fred Astaire, owned some useful hoofers of his own - horses like Social Evening, High Gat, Nick The Greek, Mavis and Rainbow Tie all won for him in England while Triplicate and Sharp Curve both landed big wins for him in the US.

Showbiz tycoon Lord Bernard Delfont was a keen racehorse owner, but he finally decided the time had come to quit the sport when his trainer told him one of his horses was crazy. 'When a jumper I had wouldn't take a fence, the trainer seriously told me the horse would need psychiatric treatment. I knew that was enough and got out.'

Bing Crosby was a part-owner of 1965 Derby runner-up Meadow Court.

Singer Frankie Vaughan found himself drawn to the world of racehorses when trainer Doug Marks wrote to him to say that he was a Vaughan fan and 'a brilliant trainer of horses'. 'It was such nonsense' said Vaughan 'I had no thought of getting involved, but I invited him to my show at the Palladium and we hit it off immediately. Doug said that he had a lovely little two-year-old that he wanted to call Jazz Singer that was crying out for a daddy. The price was exorbitant. Marks suggested that Vaughan share the horse so he contacted friends Jimmy Tarbuck, Edmundo Ross and Danny La Rue. 'It was an unlikely looking quartet but with horses like Razzamataz and Water Rat we had some wonderful times,' added Vaughan.

Beatle Paul McCartney attended Aintree races for the first time in 1966 and proudly led in the winner of the 6 furlong Hutton Plate - Drake's Drum, the horse he had bought for his father.

Actress Lily Langtry was a keen racegoer and owner. She owned two Cesarewitch winners - Merman in 1897 and Yentoi in 1908.

'Likely Lad' actor James Bolam owned jumper Credo's Daughter.

Bookmaker's son turned actor, Albert Finney had a problem. His horse Synastry was set to run in the Kentucky Derby - but Finney was due to appear in the theatre that day. Finney wanted to see the horse run so he decided to buy every seat in the theatre, reimburse the bar for its loss of profit, and buy six Concorde tickets to fly himself and friends over to see the race - all of which would set him back a cool £25,000. In the event Synastry was sidelined through injury.

When star ventriloquist Roger de Courcey went into horse ownership he didn't reckon on the problems he'd face with his horse Nookie Bear - named after his famous stage partner. His first problem came when Nookie Bear won at 14–1. Roger was on holiday and didn't have a penny on the horse. Then the second problem arose when Nookie Bear 'half-won' a race, being declared a dead-heater at a course with no photo-finish equipment. The fuming De Courcey, who had backed the horse in some hefty bets and was convinced he'd won, was so incensed that he told me he had considered buying a Polaroid camera and sending it to the judge, before thinking better of it. Then Nookie Bear gave him more problems - by nearly winning a race. De Courcey couldn't make it to Windsor to see the horse run and sent some friends along, including comedian Jim Davidson. He advised them not to back the horse, who started at 33–1. 'As they came over the last, he was in front and Jim told me later they were calling me all the names under the sun. Fortunately, he finished second and saved my life!'

Tommy Cannon (of Cannon and Ball fame) owned Cannon's Way, who won his first three outings.

Writer Charlotte Bingham owns several horses, including one named after her best seller, *To Hear A Nightingale*. And she says that her horses have brought her more attention than her writing. 'People stop me and say, "It is you, isn't it?". I light up, immediately thinking they've been reading one of my books or watching one of my television series. Then they say, "It's Fredwell's owner, isn't it?".' Fredwell has been her most successful horse, winning a dozen jump races.

Former Pink Floyd star Roger Walters owns sprinter Young Inca and a 490,000 Irish guinea purchase, Northern Hal.

'Lady in Red' star Chris de Burgh named another of his horses after his hit song 'Missing You'.

Airline tycoon Sir Freddie Laker owned 1965 Triumph Hurdle winner, Blarney Beacon.

Page Three girl Samantha Fox went into ownership with a horse called Touch Me.

Ronnie Wood, guitarist with the Rolling Stones, bought two-year-old Alchiea in 1989.

TV personality and keen race-goer Henry Kelly owned jumper Kellys Insurance, which came in a winner at Worcester in September 1988.

Commentator Peter O'Sullevan has owned many good horses, among them Triumph Hurdle winner Attivo and top sprinter Be Friendly.

Rock superstar Sting was talked into racehorse ownership by a gang of Irish builders. 'I had the builders in my house and we got talking - Sting, they said, what you need is a whole string of racehorses.' And they just happened to have one to sell him! It was called Sweetcal and went on to land some nice wins for Sting, notably at odds of 33-1 and 14-1.

Lady Rothermere: 'To be there in the owners' enclosure, watching your horse win, is the biggest thrill going.'

Percy Sugden of Coronation Street, otherwise known as Bill Waddington owns a horse called Lucy Lastic - the name was inspired by the racing phrase, 'They're off'.

TIPSTER

When he was a radio presenter, Terry Wogan featured a spot in his show called Wogan's Wager, in which he tipped horses. In three successive days a William Hill punter staked £20,000, £25,000 and £25,000 on the Wogan's Wager tip, on each occasion not even knowing which horse he was backing. The horses won at 5-2, 2-1 and 9–2, making the punter about £250,000. He never even sent Wogan a letter of thanks.

Actress Joan Collins was refused entry to the Royal Enclosure at Ascot when an eagle-eyed gateman spotted that she was wearing someone else's identity badge. Joan later told the Daily Express, 'I did it as a dare. It cost me £100 but it was great fun. And I don't give a damn.'

Eccentric politician Screaming Lord (David) Sutch was so pleased when he discovered that there was a two-year-old running in the 1989 Flat season called Lord David S, that he wrote to the horse's connections asking them whether they would consider allowing him to appoint the horse Shadow Sports Minister for his Official Monster Raving Loony Party.

He may have become famous for the little ukelele he carried in his hand,

but comedian-singer George Formby could have become even better known for the little whip he carried in his hand. For George was an apprentice jockey in the stable of trainer T Schofield in 1915, and he was riding in Ireland until 1919 when he weighed 6st 5lb.

What is the world-famous cook Mrs Beeton's link with racing? She lived in the original Epsom grandstand; her step-father was Clerk of the Course there.

Former pop star Davy Jones of the Monkees is a keen amateur jockey, whose ambition is to take part in the Grand National.

JOCKEYS

Most jockeys are desperately keen to win when they ride a fancied horse, but few are able to go to the lengths that Bertie Short of the Indian Police did when he was due to partner the heavily backed War Eagle at Dehra Din, India in 1873. Short arranged for two of his policemen to be on duty at every fence around the course to catch his horse should he fall or be unseated and warned them that on no account should they catch anyone else's. Short also hired a well known professional jockey of the day, Dignum, and stationed him in the middle of the course on a hack to take Short's place should he fall and be injured. When the race started, the main danger to Short's horse fell at the second and David Papillon, the top amateur of the day who was riding it called to the policemen to catch it. He was promptly treated to a smart salute, a broad smile and a resolute refusal by the officers to move an inch. War Eagle duly obliged.

NOT ACCORDING TO PLAN

Coming to the last hurdle in a race at Fairyhouse, Ireland in 1989, Sizzling Slave made a mistake and unseated jockey Pat Connell. As Connell hit the ground his legs tripped up Sizzling Slave and brought him down. Sadly, the horse was fatally injured.

Jockey J Sharp missed out on a winning ride on Thormanby in the 1860 Derby, thanks to his love of the bottle. Brought over from Russia to ride the 4–1 shot, Sharp managed to elude his 'minder' on the morning of the race and informed the lady of the house where he was staying that he felt faint after wasting to make the riding weight. He asked for a medicinal brandy and was given half a pint, which he promptly drank. Sharp was 'jocked off' by Harry Custance, who duly won the race.

During the 1920s, eccentric owner-trainer-rider Frank Barbour fell during the course of a race in Ireland. Instead of walking disconsolately back, he set off for a nearby road, hitched himself a lift into a nearby town, caught a train to Dublin where, still in the same clothes he wore during the race, he caught a boat and sailed to New York.

Just as he was about to make a challenge on The Pouncer at Stratford in 1964, jockey Terry Biddlecombe dropped his whip. His shouted offer to pay a tenner for a loan of anyone ele's produced no response – so Biddlecombe reached across to the nearest rider, grabbed his whip out of his hand and used it to drive The Pouncer up for a head victory.

Jockey Anthony Charlton finished first at Devon in August 1986 – unfortunately his horse finished second. Charlton and Amantiss parted company when the jockey suddenly tumbled out of the saddle as they cruised up to the finishing post. The race was awarded to the runner-up, Slip Up!

Former National Hunt champion jockey Terry Biddlecombe was once riding in a novice chase at Wincanton when he and another horse and jockey took a fence together. Biddlecombe and mount negotiated the obstacle safely but the other pair parted company, the horse doing a somersault and the jockey being catapulted on to the back of Biddlecombe's mount. 'My horse was slow enough with one jockey on his back, so it was one shove and my uninvited partner was off again,' recalled Biddlecombe.

Apprentice jockey John Carr saw the chance of glory as he rode his horse to victory at Catterick in July 1989. Unfortunately, though John and his mount Earth Spacer shot past the post first and began to pull up, the rest of the field carried on – they'd gone three furlongs of the 13 furlong race. 'I feel like putting a gun to my head' said Carr later.

Willie Carson arrived in the paddock at Newmarket ready to ride a horse for Lady Beaverbrook. Several minutes later when all the other jockeys had mounted their horses he suddenly realised that he didn't actually have a ride in the race.

Captain Nicholas Beaumont, Clerk of the Course at Ascot, still recalls the occasion in the paddock there when 'I heard a bit of commotion and there was Lester Piggott trying to get up one side of a grey horse with a very worried little apprentice trying to get up from the other side. It was actually the apprentice's mount. I think Lester had been talking and had walked across knowing that he had to ride a grey horse – but there were two in the race.'

Newmarket based jockey Paul D'Arcy went to India to ride in the 1985 Calcutta Derby – and ended up fleeing for his life. 'All the stable lads went on strike so the horses failed to turn up for the first few races on Derby day. Racegoers who had paid to get in were kept in the dark about what was happening.

'When Turf Club officials finally announced that racing was cancelled some of the crowd went wild. They started throwing chairs and TV sets around. It looked nasty so I jumped

into a taxi and left quickly for the first flight home.'

Ironside is probably the only horse to have won a race whilst ridden by a jockey with a broken leg. He did so at York in August 1786 – jockey Benjamin Smith was kicked by another runner at the start of the race.

Former jockey Jack Leach recalled watching a steeplechase in France during which the champion jump jockey of the day, called Herve, fell at the third last only to climb to his feet, somewhat dazed, and grab hold of a passing horse. He scrambled aboard and proceeded to ride it into fourth place; only afterwards was it pointed out that this was a bay horse and he'd started out on a grey one!

Billy Turner, best known as the trainer of the great American horse Seattle Slew, began his career as a steeplechase jockey. He had to struggle against putting on too much weight and on one occasion found himself needing to lose 17lbs very quickly in order to ride a particular horse. He had heard tales that in the past jockeys had lost weight by being buried in manure pits so, says Don Clippinger, Editor of Kentu-ky's *The Thoroughbred Record*, 'the rider wrapped himself in a plastic sheet and had his colleagues (at the stable) bury him in the manure pile and put a cardboard box over his head to ward off the flies. Everyone then went about their normal business and forgot about him. By the time he had had enough of his reducing system, Turner was too weak to extricate himself from the pile, so he remained there until feeding time. Trainer Burly Cocks finally said, "Who left that box on the muck pile?" They pulled Turner, barely conscious, from the pile in a hurry. "I couldn't see when they got me out," he said. He

also had a 105 degree temperature until he restored his body fluids. The reducing system worked, although he never tried it again. On that one afternoon he lost 19lbs.'

Former champion jump jockey Fred Winter pulled off one of the most extraordinary victories of all when he landed the top French race, the Grand Steeplechase de Paris in 1962, on Mandarin. After just four fences the horse's bit broke in half and Winter was forced to negotiate the rest of the course without any control or ability to steer the horse.

INJURIES

Everyone knows jump jockeys have to live with the ever present threat of injury – but as only the major injuries make headlines, perhaps we don't realise the sheer volume of injuries which beset the average jump jock. Phil Tuck, one of the leading jockeys, also considers himself one of the luckier ones when it comes to injury problems, yet he revealed in the *Sporting Life* a rundown of his injuries and the time out of action they cost him. They make an extraordinary catalogue of pain and problems:

2.5.77 Southwell - injured bone in foot - 4 days off.
14.12.77 Southwell - concussion, facial injuries - 12 days off.
28.8.79 Southwell - broken bone in foot - 23 days.
1.12.79 Market Rasen - concussion - 9 days.
20.2.80 Catterick - bruised shoulder - 5 days.
12.11.80 Sedgefield - concussion - 6 days.
27.12.80 Wetherby - multiple bruising - 16 days.
21.1.82 Catterick - badly bruised thumb - 2 days.
17.4.82 Ayr - chest injuries (coughing blood) - 17 days.
12.5.82 Concussion - 7 days.
18.1.83 Sedgefield - badly shaken - 3 days.
21.1.83 Catterick - bruised left thigh, left side of face, gums - 1 day.
17.3.83 Cheltenham - lower back injuries - 5 days.
10.10.83 Ayr - bronchial spasm - 2 days.
23.10.83 Dislocated left ring finger lunging horse at home - 19 days.
3.1.84 Ayr - lacerations to face - 7 days.
21.2.84 Sedgefield - fractured nose - 17 days.
14.4.84 Perth - bruised back - 9 days.
27.4.84 Hexham - leg injury - 5 days.
10.9.84 Hexham - fractured right collarbone - 15 days.
29.9.84 Carlisle - refractured right collarbone - 7 days.
1.5.85 Flu - 2 days.
11.5.85 Stratford - right shoulder muscle injury - 1 day.
1.6.85 Market Rasen - right shoulder injury - last day of season.
5.10.85 Kelso - broken bone in left hand - 17 days.
1.11.85 Wetherby - bruised hand - 1 day.
7.2.87 Wetherby - dazed - 2 days.
24.2.87 Sedgefield - back injury - 1 day.
23.5.87 Cartmel - dazed - 2 days.
7.1.88 Edinburgh - bruised neck - 6 days.
15.3.88 Cheltenham - suspected fractured collarbone - 10 days.
4.4.88 Wetherby - bruised back - 1 day.
6.4.88 Kelso - abdominal injury - 1 day.
7.4.88 Liverpool - neck injuries - 7 days.
21.10.88 Carlisle - internal bruising - 5 days.
30.11.88 Hexham - broken left arm - 56 days.

One injury not listed here which happened to Phil was perhaps the most bizarre of his career, although the effects were fairly short-lived. Phil had ridden two winners at Cartmel and was standing in the winners' enclosure when waitress Chrissie Kent crept up behind him, sank her teeth into his breeches and bit him, leaving a smudge of lipstick and a row of teeth marks on his backside. It was her way of showing her appreciation for his efforts with the two winners, which she had backed, she later admitted. Commented Phil, 'I can think of better ways of showing gratitude.' Major Tim Riley, Clerk of the Course at Cartmel, added 'As a general rule, we cannot have people going into the winners' enclosure and biting the jockeys' arses.'

Chris Warren had been counting the days to his comeback after having been off the course for five weeks with a broken collar bone. His comeback ride was on Allied Force in a novice hurdle at Newbury on Saturday 26 November, 1988. On the morning of the race he discovered that his car had been stolen overnight and left wrecked several miles away. Chris had to dash to the car where, fortunately, his riding gear had been left intact. By the time he cadged a lift to Newbury he was late - another jockey was already in his colours ready to ride. Chris changed in a flash and dashed into the parade ring in time to mount Allied Force. Allied Force fell at the first and as Chris fell he smashed the same collar bone.

Australian jockey Fred Dummett had more than his fair share of injury problems too. He fractured his right thigh three times, broke all of his ribs, his foot, his leg, his wrist, his collar bone - 29 times - and had a cartilage removed.

It was the ambulanceman who had to be transported back in his own vehicle when Jeremy Hindley, then a jockey now a trainer, took a fall at Fakenham only to then cannon into the nearby medic, breaking that gentleman's leg in the process.

After falling from his mount, Calyx, at Musselburgh, Scotland in 1879, jockey Tom Bruckshaw was taken to hospital and was later a little surprised to read of his death in the evening paper. He lived to be 90, and died peacefully in his sleep.

Jockey A Watson, riding Clem in a 6 furlong sprint at Trentham, New Zealand in July 1911, broke his leg - when it hit a spectator leaning over the inside rail in the home straight.

Gerald Foljambe had a leg amputated below the knee, but still rode a steeplechase double at Melton, Leicester in 1925.

RECORDS, FIRSTS AND ACHIEVEMENTS

Jockey Chris Antley hit a real winning streak from early February to late April 1989 at the Aqueduct track in America. He rode a winner there on 64 successive racing days.

In 1905 Elijah Wheatley was champion jockey on the Flat whilst still an apprentice.

Johnny Wairoa rode a winner in 1929 in New Zealand - but had to wait until the 1950–51 season for his next one, Merry Crooner at Poverty Bay. He had been inactive because of injury during most of that period.

In 1921, 18-year-old Harry Wragg, then an apprentice, rode the winner of the first race of the season, Glenaster, and the winner of his final race on the last day of the season, Knee Cap.

In September 1764 jockey Joseph Rose rode at three different meetings, Manchester, Richmond (Yorks) and Lincoln on consecutive days, commuting between each meeting on his own horse, carrying his racing saddle on his back.

Harry Beasley rode Mollie in the Corinthian Plate at Baldoyle, Dublin in June 1935 and was unplaced. Harry was 83, the oldest jockey ever to compete in a race. The youngest jockey was probably Australian Frank Wootton, who rode winners in South Africa at the age of 9. Victor Morley Lawson rode his first winner, Ocean King at Warwick, when he was 67.

The lowest total of winners by a champion Flat jockey was Steve Donoghue's 42 in 1917. Gordon Richards' 269 in 1947 is the highest. Over jumps the figures are R Smith's 12 in 1941–42 and Peter Scudamore's 221 in 1988–89.

Terry Biddlecombe was the first National Hunt jockey to ride 100 winners in consecutive seasons. He did it in 1965 and 1966.

Sir Gordon Richards was the first jockey to be knighted.

Who was the first Scottish champion jockey? Willie Carson, in 1972.

Stuart Shilston became the first jockey to take part in the London Marathon when he competed in the 1989 event to raise money for paralysed jockey Jessica Charles-Jones.

IN THE SADDLE

American jockey Tod Sloan, who came to England in 1897, caused a sensation here with his 'monkey on a stick' style of riding. Initially ridiculed, his success with the method - he rode 254 winners from just 801 mounts - soon revolutionised the upright style of riding preferred at the time by British jockeys. Sloan had based his technique on that of bareback negro riders from the American South. His own love of a gamble eventually cost him his licence and he died in 1933 in the charity ward of a Los Angeles hospital.

Nineteenth century jockey Freddie Hobson had an eccentric style in the saddle. Every time he jumped a fence he would grab hold of the back of his saddle. Asked why, he explained that it reduced the weight on the horse's forelegs as it landed, and he had the last laugh when he won the 1877 Grand National on Austerlitz.

Black jockeys have always been few and far between in Britain, but in America they played a vital role in shaping early Turf history and continue to flourish. 14 out of the 15 riders in the first Kentucky Derby (1875) were black, and black riders won 15 of that race's first 28 runnings. Perhaps the greatest black jockey was Isaac Murphy, the first man to win 3 Kentucky Derbies, in 1884, 1890 and 1891. He also had a remarkable career record of 44% success.

One of the greatest near-miss stories of all must belong to jockey H. Barker who, in 1893, finished runner-up in both the Grand National and in the Derby (on Ravensbury).

Jockey Tommy Pickernell was so successful as an amateur rider in Tasmania, where he had emigrated to from Cheltenham in the early 1850s, that the local paid riders instigated a petition calling on him to stop 'taking the bread from the mouths of professional jockeys'. Pickernell took the hint and returned to England where he rode hundreds of winners before his death in 1912.

He never got the chance to say 'I told you so', but jockey Arthur Yates warned his friend and fellow jockey George Ede, 'Don't ride the brute, he'll kill you' just before Ede partnered Chippenham in the 1870 Sefton Chase at Aintree. Ede was killed when Chippenham fell at the fence before the water jump.

The Stewards at Huntingdon couldn't believe their own ears when they inquired into the dreadful running of Hello Rocky, who jumped atrociously before falling at the fourth in a novice hurdle race there in February 1989. Jockey Barrie Wright told them that the horse was deaf and that this had contributed to his appalling performance, adding, 'I nearly fell off at the first and nearly fell off at the second. So when I eventually did go it was really quite a relief.'

In an era when the honesty of jockeys was not always above reproach – the 1930s – Australian Rae Johnstone proved himself to be probably the most genuine and trustworthy of them all. He asked a confidante to place 10,000 francs for him on the favourite in a race in France in which Johnstone was riding an outsider. Johnstone then proceeded to ride an inspired race on the outsider to get up on the line to beat the favourite.

Legendary champion jockey Sir Gordon Richards had his first mount in public in 1920 – thanks to a football match! Gordon was a stable lad at Jimmy White's stables in Wiltshire and was playing right-back for the stable soccer team who were 3–3 with minutes to go when they were awarded a penalty. White called out that if Gordon took the penalty and scored he'd give him his first ride in a proper racc. He scored – and rode Clockwork into fourth place at Lingfield shortly after.

John Francome made one of the most sporting gestures ever seen in the 1981–82 National Hunt season. Peter Scudamore had been leading the race for the jockey championship when he fell and was badly injured. Francome continued to ride until he drew level with Scudamore; then he retired for the season, leaving the championship shared between them.

In November 1873 champion jockey Fred Archer rode Stirling to win the Liverpool Autumn Cup. The horse's trainer, T Roughton, was so pleased that he gave Archer a present – a short-barrelled gun. Archer later took his own life with that gun, almost 13 years to the day later.

Jockey and trainer Arthur Goodwill was universally known as 'Fiddler' – not because he was crooked or dishonest, but because the day he arrived at Jack Leader's stables to become an apprentice he was carrying a violin.

Puerto Rican jockey Pedro Juan Vinales might well have strong claims to be considered the sport's leading loser, or so Irwin M Tress, Senior Vice President of the El Commandante track in that country, felt when he told me of Pedro's record. 'Pedro raced over a period of five years at El Commandante,' said Mr Tress. 'During this time he raced more than 90 times and finally he won one race in 1962, after which he promptly retired.'

Modesty was not Sam Chifney's strong point. The jockey who rode five Classic winners wrote in his autobiography, 'In 1773 I could ride horses in a better manner than any person ever known in my time. In 1775 I could train horses for running better than any person I ever yet saw.' Modest or not he met a sad end, dying in a debtors' prison having failed to settle a £350 bill for a saddle.

Jockey John Mangle, who won the St Leger five times during the late 18th century, was known as Crying Jackie, for his habit of bursting into tears whenever he was beaten.

Greville Starkey became known as The Barker for his frequent habit of launching into dog imitations at the slightest excuse.

MONEY MATTERS

During the thirteen consecutive years in which he was champion jockey, Fred Archer's retainers, riding fees and presents from owners earned him an estimated £100,000. During his career, Archer's usual daily diet consisted of warm castor oil, dry toast and half a glass of champagne.

Archer was also famous for being 'careful' with money. A favourite trick was to ask a bystander for the loan of a few coins to put in his waistband to make up his weight as he went to the scales - which he would then 'forget' to return.

But the stories about Lester Piggott take some beating. Northern trainer Mick Easterby claims to be the only trainer who ever got away without giving Lester a present for riding a winner for him. Easterby, who is also a farmer, described how Piggott rode Valarion to win for him at Pontefract after which Easterby pleaded poverty, to which Lester responded 'Can't you manage a bag of spuds?'

The first jockey to receive an annual retainer of £5000 in a season was Nat Flatman in 1848.

Desperate to sell his house during a slump in property prices in September 1989, jockey Dean McKeown offered prospective purchasers the incentive of a half-share in a two-year-old due to run the following season.

Champion jockey Pat Eddery's glittering career was nearly over before it started when, at the age of four, he was flung out of a car being driven at 60mph by his father Jimmy, after a friend had failed to shut the door properly. Pat survived with cuts and bruises.

Legendary American jockey Bill Shoemaker was born premature in 1931 and was allegedly incubated in a shoebox by his grandmother.

A jockey called Kitchener reputedly weighed 3st 7lbs when he won the 1844 Chester Cup. Four years earlier when he rode at Ascot his weight was reported to be 2st 1lb.

IN GEAR

Having finished down the field in a race in Zurich, jockey Richard Fox was accused by the owner of his mount of having ridden like a cowboy - Fox could hardly disagree, he'd arrived at the course with too light a saddle and the President of the racecourse had loaned him a genuine cowboy saddle 'with horn and everything'.

John Wells, who rode Pero Gomez to win the 1869 St Leger, turned up a couple of days before to ride the horse in a training gallop wearing an Alpine hat with several feathers, a suit made from a Gordon plaid, and a pair of red morocco slippers.

After remaining virtually unchanged for years, jockey silks began to undergo a transformation in the late 1980s when aerodynamic silks, modelled on athletes' outfits, were introduced with the designers claiming the skin hugging outfits would save a jockey up to three yards a mile because of lower wind resistance.

NAMES

Some famous jockey's nicknames:
Fred Archer
The Tin Man
Lester Piggott
The Long Fella
Steve Cauthen
The Kentucky Kid
Harry Wragg
The Head Waiter
Sir Gordon Richards
The Champ or *Moppy*, because of his thick black hair.
Joe Mercer
Smokin' Joe - he was runner-up in the Pipe Smoker of the Year contest in 1979.
Frank Buckle
Pocket Hercules or *Peterborough Screw*

'*Cash*' Asmussen's first name is Brian.

The middle names of Royal trainer Captain Peter Hastings Bass are Robin Hood.

One of the more appropriate racing names belongs to a bookie named Stallion.

The Queen likes to name her own horses, and she comes up with some appropriate names - in 1989 she named a colt by Rainbow Quest out of Soprano, Son Et Lumiere.

Owner Gordon Shaw claims he named a filly of his after his wife Pam - the filly's name? My Ratbag.

Jockey Club chiefs didn't realise just how risque they were being when they allowed City whizz kid Alan Tappin, 32, from Essex, to name his 1989 two-year-old Who Gives A Donald - inspired by a cockney rhyming slang expression for a rude word rhyming with Donald Duck. Commented Jockey Club official David Pipc, 'We don't have many experts in rhyming slang.'

No one could be offended by Michael Proudlock and Rex Leyland's horse's name, Foxtrot Oscar, could they? Only if they knew that in the language of pilots and police officers, Foxtrot Oscar is a slang expression for '________ off'!

It occasionally happens to a horse that only one of his testicles drops - this affliction has been known to inspire those responsible for naming the animals - hence Masked Ball, Oneupmanship and Something's Missing.

Cacoethes, third in the 1989 Derby, was originally given the name Our Friend Elvis, as a yearling.

Gainsborough, the first Derby winner (1917) to be owned by a woman, Lady James Douglas, was not, as is popularly supposed, named after the famous painter. In fact, her Ladyship chose the name by picking up a railway guide and going through it until she came upon a name she liked, which happened to be that of a town in Lincolnshire, Gainsborough.

The name of an 1846 Grand National runner was Hornihiharriho - very few people could pronounce this and he was popularly known as Hurry Harry.

Running names together seems to be very popular in America these days as some recent examples show - Agirlfrommars runs at Santa Anita, the Canadian Derby was won by Haveigotadealforu, while Doyouseewhatisee and Akissforjose both won during the 1989 Flat season. Perhaps the oddest of these names is that of a Ruidoso Downs winner, Hookinonthehighway.

Names in use during the domestic 1989 Flat season included Afrienddroppingin and Motherubbadscubbad.

OWNERS

Owner Dorothy Paget, who had 1532 winners during her connection with the Turf, including the 1943 Derby winner Straight Deal, was a reclusive and eccentric figure. It was said that at Christmas she didn't put sixpences in the Pudding but filled the mince pies with cheques!

Her bookmaker obviously had every confidence in her honesty. As she was in the habit of working at night and sleeping all day, he would allow her to back her horses in the evening even if they had run earlier that day, trusting her not to have discovered the results.

Dorothy also had an unusual method of deciding her betting stakes - if someone rang her up on the morning of a race she would discover their phone number then stake that number in pounds on her runner.

When Dorothy's chauffeur-driven car broke down, making her late for a race meeting during the Second World War, she vowed it would never happen again - so she made sure that in future a spare car followed behind whenever she went to the races.

Horatio Bottomley was realistic enough to know that his 1907 Derby entry, John Bull, wouldn't win the race. But that didn't stop him devising a plan to make sure that the horse got noticed and promoted his magazine, also called John Bull. So Bottomley instructed his jockey, James Hare Junior, to ride the horse along in front for as far as possible – and the next day he had advertising placards printed reading 'John Bull leads the field.'

Bottomley once decided to teach the Belgians a lesson by entering six of his useful horses in a minor race at the Blankenberg course. The plan was that he would bet varying amounts under different names on each horse with only the jockeys knowing who should finish where. Everything went smoothly – until the race started and a thick sea mist drifted over the course, leaving the jockeys unable to see what was going on. They finished up in completely the wrong order and Bottomley lost a fortune.

William Douglas, Earl of March and Ruglen and fourth Duke of Queensbury was better known as Old Q and was reckoned to be one of his age's most outrageous roisterers. On one occasion, shortly before a race, his jockey came to him to reveal that he had been offered a large sum of money to pull his mount. Old Q instructed the jockey to accept the bribe. Later, as he helped to saddle the horse Old Q suddenly announced, 'I think I'll ride this myself', removing the long coat he always wore to reveal himself clad in his own racing colours. To the amusement of his jockey and the dismay of the would-be bribers, Old Q and his mount duly won the race.

After they failed to reach their reserve price of 15,000 guineas at the Newmarket Sales, owner-breeder Stephen Forsyth struck a private deal to sell two yearlings for £10,000 each. He was not, to put it mildly, best pleased when Never So Bold went on to win the Kings Stand Stakes at Royal Ascot and Newmarket's July Cup in 1985 and Commanche Run won the 1984 St Leger.

Jumper Recollect runs for a syndicate of owners called the Bow Tie Club. When the horse wins, the winners' enclosure resembles a Frank Muir look-alike convention.

Racehorse owner John Finney planned to name a horse after a bookmaker friend, Bob Menzies, but as that was also the name of a former Australian Prime Minister the Jockey Club wouldn't allow it, so a compromise was reached with Menzie's Flyer.

When he died, the ashes of Tony Stratton-Smith, record business executive, racehorse owner and sponsor, were scattered over the last hurdle at Newbury – or should have been. Recalls Stratton-Smith's partner Chris Wright, 'A rather nervous Philippa Kindersley (wife of their trainer, Gay) somehow managed to get downwind of the ashes and most of them ended up on her rather than over the hurdle.'

Henry, third Marquis of Waterford was a legendary owner, rider and gambler of the mid-nineteenth century. Henry it was, apparently who originated the term 'painting the town red' as he and his friends would do just that after enjoying a good night out. One of his most famous exploits is celebrated by sporting artist Henry Allen in a print whose caption reads, 'The Noble Marquis on his celebrated hunter Don Juan, jumping a five-barred gate in a drawing-room in Melton for a bet of 100 guineas at half past 10 o'clock at night in December, with a blazing fire staring him in the face.'

Frenchman the Prince de Conde built a magnificent stable, the Grandes Ecuries at Chantilly, for his fine string of racehorses during the eighteenth century. But he did have a good reason for so doing as he was convinced that after he died he would be reincarnated as a racehorse and he wanted to make sure he would be well accomodated.

In 1984 Robert Sangster's horses were trained by eleven English trainers, six in Ireland, two in France, fifteen in Australia, six in America and eight in South Africa.

John Bowes, who would have been Earl of Strathmore had his father not neglected to marry his mother until he, the son, was nine years old, owned many useful horses - including Derby winners Daniel O'Rourke and West Australian. Yet Bowes was such a reclusive character that George Fordham, who was his jockey for over thirty years, only ever saw him twice.

Lord Rosslyn and Mr Clayton haggled over the price of an injured filly, and Lord Rosslyn finally bought Atalanta for 7/6d (37½p), a wheelbarrow and a free nomination to one of Rosslyn's pigs for Clayton's prize sow. Atalanta became the dam of Ayrshire, who won the 1888 Derby.

It is difficult to decide whether Bower Ismay was one of the luckiest racehorse owners or one of the unluckiest. He was a major shareholder in the White Star Line and sailed on the maiden voyage of their new vessel - The Titanic. He survived and then saw the realisation of every owner's dream when his Craganour, a hot favourite, won the 1913 Derby - only to be disqualified in favour of a 100–1 chance.

Another contender for the Unluckiest Owner title must be Lord Astor, who owned five runners-up in the seven Derbies between 1918 and 1924.

Lord Howard de Walden, owner of Derby winner Slip Anchor and the top class Kris amongst many others, and three times Senior Steward of the Jockey Club, revealed how he nearly changed the course of history many years ago when, whilst driving a car in Germany, he knocked someone over. 'I was driving very slowly but as I didn't speak any German I asked the chap I was with to see if the fellow was all right. After we'd established that he was unharmed and gone on our way, my companion told me that I'd knocked down a man called Adolf Hitler who had just formed a political party and was beginning to make an impression on the German political scene.' Asked whether he thought he should have been driving faster, the philosophical Lord answered, 'I doubt whether it would have made any long term difference to the course of history;

someone else would probably have come along to take over from Hitler.'

Few people would associate Hitler with horse racing, but it is said that the German dictator met with the Aga Khan when that great racing supporter visited Germany in October 1937. The two discussed the Aga's racing interests and Hitler asked how much a good stallion would be worth. The Aga Khan, owner of five Derby winners, told Hitler that the value would be some £30,000, whereupon Hitler asked whether he would exchange one stallion for thirty cars. According to legend the Aga Khan replied, 'What would I do with them? I don't want to open a motor shop in Piccadilly.'

One of the interesting features of the racing scene in the mid-to-late nineteenth century was a proliferation of 'racing parsons', one of the most notable of whom was the Rev John King, who ran his horses under the name of Mr Launde, although this subterfuge fooled few. In one season alone the Rev King won the St Leger, won £15,000 in stake money, argued with his Bishop and resigned his position. He died in 1875, causing controversy even then. Because of his demise, his much fancied colt Holy Friar was unable to compete in the Derby for which it was ante-post favourite.

When the Reverend Colville Wallis of St Agnes Church in Newmarket offered up prayers for fine weather to prevent damage to the harvest which was being caused by rain he was unaware that the Lady of the Manor, Caroline, Duchess of Montrose was in the congregation. The late-nineteenth-century lady was a keen racehorse owner and she had a live St Leger hope which needed soft going. Upon hearing the Reverend's prayers she stormed out of the church and later informed him that if he insisted on arranging for fine weather before the St Leger he could find another church to do it in.

In the late nineteenth century a Melbourne journalist named 'Braddy' Bradshaw kept his racehorse in the kitchen as he couldn't afford stabling fees.

Dunbar was a minor Scottish meeting held between 1871 and 1906. A gentleman farmer from Berwick, Mr J Calder, achieved a certain notoriety when at one meeting he owned, rode and trained every single winner. He was subsequently debarred by the race committee from entering horses there on the grounds that he was spoiling the meeting.

Scottish owner James Merry was elected to Parliament in 1859, representing a highly puritanical constituency which was up in arms when it discovered that Mr Merry had allowed one of his horses to go to France to run on a Sunday, and that it had won. He was summoned to a meeting of outraged constituents demanding an explanation. The way he got out of his little problem revealed him to be a consummate politician. According to an observer, he said, 'It is quite true that having sent a horse of mine to run on the continent, I did so far forget myself as to conform to the customs of the country in which I was staying and allowed him to start for an important prize on the Sabbath day,' (loud groans from all over the hall). 'But, gentlemen, I must add that before I thought about the day on which the race was to be run I had backed my horse very heavily with the French and I won their money and brought it all back to spend in Scotland.' 'Straightaway' reports the observer, 'all those in the room felt their hearts touched, and waving their bonnets they joined in three cheers for the member and then departed singing *Auld Lang Syne*.'

There can have been few stranger, more eccentric owners of racehorses than the Earl of Glasgow, who died in 1869. He would frequently argue at length with the expert handicapper Admiral Rous, because he felt his horses had been given too little weight to carry in handicap races! The Earl once persuaded the Admiral to add a whole stone to one of his runner's weights, and was delighted when it was beaten by just a short head. He hated naming his horses and many ran without names, while others were called 'He Has A Name', 'Give Him A Name' and 'He Isn't Worth A Name'. If he felt his horses were no good he would have them shot. On the final day of a meeting at Houghton in 1862 he ran six horses, announcing that they would all be shot should they fail to win. A huge crowd turned out for the 'Do or Die' events, and all six won, to escape execution. The Earl once threw a waiter through a window, telling the manager, 'Put him on the bill'. The Earl had very little luck with his horses and won few valuable prizes, yet when a friend once sympathised after a defeat, he snapped: 'Be sorry for yourself, not me. I have £60,000 a year and can afford to lose – you cannot.'

Recalling one of his most memorable days as a trainer, when five of his horses won on the same day at Wolverhampton in 1968, Ken Oliver said that by the time the last winner, Shingle Bay, was being led back to the unsaddling enclosure by winning owner Agnes Ogilvy, the celebrations had reached such a pitch that she fell over leading the horse in and the horse promptly fell on top of her.

Ambrose Gorham, owner of the 1902 Grand National winner Shannon Lass, used the prize money to restore the church in his village of Telscombe. On his death, he left the whole parish and village to the Brighton Corporation with the following guidelines: 'I direct the Corporation shall prefer a man who is a sportsman and not a total abstainer from alcohol and tobacco' to succeed him.

In the 1870s Lord Falmouth was the leading racehorse owner in England, but he never gambled. He broke that rule on just one occasion – Mrs Scott, the wife of his trainer, bet him sixpence that his filly Queen Bertha would win the Oaks. Lord Falmouth accepted the bet – and Queen Bertha duly won the Oaks. He paid up, having the sixpence set in diamonds before presenting it to Mrs Scott.

Racehorse owner Tony McGuinness got plastered when his horse finally won a race – literally. 53-year-old Tony jumped for joy as Carramore Outlaw passed the post at Perth – then he fell flat on his back and broke a bone.

Dr Paddy Morrissey, who now has a successful practice in a fashionable area of London and who owns horses trained by Mick O'Toole, was nearly lost to the medical world. 'In 1948 my mother gave me £10 as the entry fee for my final exams as a medical student. I put the money on the Irish horse, Prince Regent, in the Gold Cup. It won at 6-4 on. If it had lost I'd never have become a doctor.'

The Duke of Portland was an important owner in the late eighteenth and early nineteenth century, but trainer Fred Darling decided that he no longer wanted to train the Duke's horses - because he was irritated by his habit of cracking his knuckles!

In 1920 Lord Glanely, a former Cardiff shipping clerk, broke the record price for a yearling by paying 14,500 guineas for Blue Ensign - the horse never won a race.

ALL IN THE FAMILY

In 1879, four brothers from the Irish Beasley family rode in the Grand National. Tommy was 3rd on Martha, Willie 8th on Lord Marcus, Harry 9th on Turco, while Johnny had to pull up on Victor II.

Twins John (Ascot Stakes - Corydalis) and Dominic (Royal Hunt Cup - Chivalry) Forte both rode a winner at Royal Ascot in 1954.

Racing fan Johnny Burns watched his brother Tommy 'TP' Burns ride to victory in the 1921 Ayr Gold Cup - and he was still there watching the race when it was run in 1989, having seen every single running of the race since that day. Johnny is 88, and brother Tommy, long since retired, still going strong at 91.

Jockey Michael Hills was riding at Ripon when his saddle slipped and he fell. At exactly the same moment, miles away at Lambourn, his twin brother Richard, also a jockey, was out riding a bike. He fell off and broke his arm.

American Lester Rieff, champion jockey of 1900, was warned off by the Jockey Club who withdrew his licence after he was found to have deliberately allowed a horse ridden by his brother John to beat his own mount, De Lacy, at a race in Manchester

Trainer Barry Hills kept his bet for the 1988 Flat season in the family - he took odds of 1000-1 for a stake of £35 that he or a member of his family would train or ride every winner on the card at a meeting. He lost.

Husband and wife raced against each other for the first time in a big Cheltenham race when Robert and Theresa Elwell both lined up in the Audi Grand Prix chase in May 1988. Theresa partnered Mister Skip into second place while Robert and his mount, White Paper, parted company at the fourteenth fence.

Trainer Jack Berry and his family set an unusual record when they all rode in public on the same day, May 30 1981. Jack rode in a race at Kempton, his wife Jo and sons Alan and Martin all at Ayr. Berry was also the first trainer to carry commercial advertising on his horse box.

It's hardly surprising that Lester Piggott became a great jockey - after all, it runs in his family. Dad Keith was a jockey and trainer and Mum, Iris Rickaby, twice won the Newmarket Town Plate. Lester's uncle, Fred Rickaby, rode three Classic winners; his grandfather, Ernest Piggott, won three Grand

Nationals; his great grandfather, Tom Cannon, won the Derby and great great grandfather, John Barham Day, rode 16 Classic winners and trained seven.

Other successful jockeys and trainers, though, are emphatically not from racing stock:

Sir Gordon Richards' father was a Shropshire miner; Steve Donoghue's was a Warrington steelworker; John Francome is the son of a builder; and Michael Stoute's father was Commissioner of Police in Barbados. As for John 'Kipper' Lynch, who raced in the sixties and seventies - his father was a fish merchant on the Old Kent Road.

In 1919 Irish trainer Bob Fetherstonhaugh was so delighted at training the Grand National runner-up Ballybogan that he decided to have his son christened in that name! His wife, however, was not so keen and after some discussion they agreed to call the boy Aintree.

What is the connection between trainer Neville Crump and custard? His wife Sylvia's grandfather, Alfred Bird, invented Bird's custard powder.

Who is trainer Peter Walwyn's favourite Bonk?
His wife, Virginia - it's her nickname.

A racing tip led to marriage for Fiona Dunkley and Steve Simkiss. Both were at Windsor races in 1984 and were unaware of each other until Yorkshireman Steve, who was in one party of people, passed on a tip to Fiona, from East Grinstead, who was there with another group. The horse lost, but Fiona and Steve had been brought together. When they wed in August 1989 they took twenty guests to a reception at the racecourse without which it would never have happened.

RACING RULES AND RULERS

THE JOCKEY CLUB

The Jockey Club came to prominence in the mid-eighteenth century. In 1752 they built a Coffee Room at Newmarket. In 1762 they published a list of registered racing colours. The first man to be expelled from the Jockey Club was Mr Brereton, 'for charging Meynell and Vernon with cheating at play' then in 1770, Mr Quick and Mr Castle were banned from running their horses and Thomas Dunn from riding them.

Until 1850 a 'Feather' was a jockey weighing around four or five stones. In 1850 the Jockey Club decided that a 'Featherweight' should be considered 4 stone. In 1858 that was raised to 4st 7lb then 5st 7lb in 1861. The term was dropped in 1876 when it was ruled that no horse should carry less than 5st 7lb. Feathers were seldom individually named on a racecard.

Daniel Dawson was hanged at Cambridge in 1812 having been convicted of poisoning racehorses. He was the only member of a gang who were out to 'stop' certain horses to be brought to justice. Bizarrely, the Jockey Club named a race at Newmarket in the 1960s the Daniel Dawson Stakes, although the move did not go down well and the race was soon renamed.

Following the victory of Speed On at Folkestone in 1935 when ridden by J Hickey, the use of rattles by jockeys was banned.

In recognition of contributions to the community, the Hong Kong Jockey Club was in 1960 granted the 'Royal' prefix by Her Majesty the Queen. The Club is a strictly non-profit-making organisation with surplus funds being given to social welfare, sports and recreation projects.

In 1988 an Australian punter, desperate to stem the tide of losers he kept backing, wrote to the Victoria Amateur Turf Club asking them to ban him from their courses.

STEWARDS AND OFFICIALS

Stewards Inquiries into racecourse disputes and controversies are commonplace today, but perhaps the first of them is recorded in a 1682 report of a race: 'Mr Griffin was appointed to start them. When he saw them equall he sayd Goe, and presently he cried out Stay. One went off, and run through the Course and claims the money, the other never stird at all. Most possibly you may say that this was not a fayre starting, but the critics say after the word Goe was out of the mouth his commission was determined, and it was illegal for him to say Stay. Tis all referred to His Majesty's judgement, who hath not yet determined it.'

Racing hasn't always been a well regulated sport, as the *Illustrated London News* pointed out in 1835. 'Up to the first quarter of this century, you went to Newmarket, where the existence of the animal you staked your money on could no more be known to you till he came to the starting post (and not then unless you had a good telescope) than the state of the Emperor of Morocco's bile. You went to Epsom, and found the jockeys starting themselves, or to Doncaster, and saw them deciding how they came in . . .'

In 1888 the Stewards of the Calcutta course were unable to deal with an appeal against one of their decisions as all the records had been eaten by white ants.

In 1824 the Duke of Richmond was the victim of one of the oddest judging decisions ever when his Dandizette won the Goodwood

Stakes – the judge, Charles Greville, was concentrating so much on the close duel between Vitellina and Ghost that he completely failed to spot Dandizette, who was racing on the other side of the course. Lord Verulam, ruled to be the winning owner, was embarrassed and offered the stakes to the Duke of Richmond, who turned the offer down, saying the race had been judged and that was an end to the matter.

Thirty minutes after a race on Easter Monday, 1986, the Hereford judge decided that he'd announced the wrong result and changed his decision. Peter Roffe-Silvester initially gave the race to Play The Knave, but the photo-finish print clearly showed even-money favourite Castle Warden was the winner. Some bookies, who had to pay out twice on the result were not best pleased. Mr Roffe-Silvester resigned some days later.

Tardy time-keeping has always been an irritation at race metings – in the late nineteenth century the powers that be came up with a novel way of dealing with the problem, issuing a public announcement that 'the Clerk of the Course at York will regulate his watch by the clock of York Cathedral, and will be fined 5s (25p) for every minute he is behind time in the bell not ringing for the respective races.'

Security men had to be introduced to the Stewards' Room at Towcester racecourse a couple of years ago after it was revealed that a number of punters had taken to pressing their ears against the rickety door of the Room in order to get advance information on the outcomes of Stewards Enquiries.

Another Clem won the last race on the card at Punchestown in April 1989, but no-one at the course backed the winner. This was because bookmakers' clerks, tote staff and the official time keeper all went on strike, objecting to the fact that the eight-race card didn't finish until 5.45.
Pickets were on duty at the 1975 1000 Guineas at Newmarket, as stable lads were on strike.

In the early twentieth century there was a Steward called Captain 'Wiggie' Weyland who was alleged to have delayed the hearing of an objection at Windsor where he was officiating, in order that he could place a bet on the outcome.

Even those racegoers who thought they'd heard every excuse in the book for a beaten horse had to admit that apprentice Darren Haw had come up with a new one when he complained that his mount had been held back by one of the stalls attendants. Riding Alecshope at Warwick Farm, Sydney towards the end of 1987, Haw was on the hot favourite but could only finish second behind Mrs A1. Following this he lodged his bizarre complaint to the stewards. The stewards carried out an investigation during which the starter, Bill Cooper, confirmed that one of the runners in the stalls had kicked out, causing Alecshope to lunge forward. Just as the attendant grabbed the horse's head to steady him so the starter hit the button to send the field on its way. The stewards officially declared Alecshope a non-runner.

Bringing his horse under orders on his first appearance in Switzerland,

jump jockey Hywel Davies' mount decided to charge the tape. 'The starter there holds the tape himself and lets go when the horses are in line,' recalls Davies. 'I thought the starter would let go for his own good, but he held on tight and was catapulted clean over the running rails.'

Jockeys are often in trouble for misuse of their whip. New Zealand jockey David Walsh got into trouble in July 1984 for riding (and winning on) Colman with two whips. The horse was a difficult ride and Walsh felt two whips would help to keep him on a straight course. Local steward Noel McCutcheon disagreed, and promptly banned the use of two whips, saying they were 'too dangerous for an inexperienced rider'.

Australian jockey Steven Maskiell must have got out of bed on the wrong side when he went to ride at Elwick, Hobart on Tasmanian Derby Day in 1989. By the end of the day Maskiell had been fined 700 Aussie dollars after a parade ring punch-up with Melbourne jockey Gary Skinner; called to an inquiry to face a charge of allegedly using his elbows and obstructing a horse's running in the third race; and fined a further one thousand dollars by the stewards for careless riding in the last race of the day.

During a career stretching from his first winner in 1904 to his last in 1937, the legendary Steve Donoghue was never once summoned before the Stewards for any misdemeanour.

Just after passing the winning post at Newton Abbot in 1974, jockey Stephen Stanhope fractured his arm when he collided with a stray horse. He was put in the course ambulance and was being driven away when a concerned punter rushed over to the vehicle and insisted that Stanhope be taken to the weighing room to ensure that he wasn't disqualified for failing to weigh in. He was taken to the weighing room, but stewards allowed him to dispense with the usual procedure.

The conditions of a race held during a meeting taking place at Calcutta in 1832 must have left competitors fagged out. For the Cheroot Stakes, which attracted a 17 strong field, it was stipulated that each rider should 'start with a lighted cheroot in his mouth, keep same alight during the race and bring it alight to the weighing place, or be considered distanced (disqualified)'. The cigar of just one rider was extinguished during the mile race.

Confusion finished first in the 1974 Queen Anne Stakes at Royal Ascot, with Gloss and Royal Prerogative second and third - but Brook, six lengths back in fourth place, won the race when the first three were all subsequently disqualified.

Trainer David Elsworth was fined £55 for sending his horse Kpjes into the paddock late for a race at Wincanton on Easter Monday 1989. In his defence Elsworth made the excuse that he'd had to stop on the way to the races so that his four-and-a-half-year-old daughter Jessica could be sick. The stewards were unimpressed by the explanation.

Horses are often disqualified for something they or their jockeys have done, but rarely for something their sire didn't do. That was the fate 'enjoyed' by Prince Of Dance who won the 1988 Washington Singer Stakes, only later to lose the race because it was for two-year-olds sired by stallions who won over at least 1½miles. His sire, Sadlers Wells won over a maximum of 1¼m.

Weighing in has always been an important feature of organised horse racing. As long ago as July 1710, Conrad von Uffenbach was writing of a meeting at Epsom: 'As soon as the fellows have dismounted and got their breath a little they are again weighed, and if one of them has lost even his whip, which must weigh half a pound, he cannot win. We were told that some time ago there was a man who, feeling unwell, had to vomit, did so in his hat and brought it back with him so that he should not be any lighter.'

The 1927 Cambridgeshire was officially judged to be a dead heat between Medal and Niantic, but many impartial and important observers at Newmarket were convinced that the horse placed third, Insight II, had actually won the race. Reported the *Daily Telegraph*, 'Most onlookers, including some of those in the Jockey Club stand were under the impression that Insight II was a clear winner,'

The 1844 Derby 'winner', Running Rein, was eventually revealed to have been Maccabaeus, a four-year-old. The race, of course, is for three-year-olds. It had been suspected before the race that Running Rein was an impostor and the Stewards had already ruled that if either he or another suspect runner, Leander, should win, the stakes would be withheld and an inquiry launched. Leander broke his leg during the race and was later destroyed, having been revealed as a six-year-old. The Ugly Buck, favourite for this extraordinary race, was deliberately 'held back' by his jockey while the second favourite, Ratan, was nobbled and pulled by his jockey. 20–1 chance Orlando, who finished second, was ultimately awarded the race.

Jamie Duff of Edinburgh discovered an interesting loophole in the rules of racing at Leith in the 18th century. Finding that there was nothing in the rules to stipulate that runners should have four legs and a tail, Duff entered himself and completed the course, whipping himself in with a stick. He finished a poor last.

'Just how old are you, Running Rein, or should I say Maccabaeus?'

THEY SAID IT

'Eclipse first, the rest nowhere' is perhaps the most famous of all racing quotes and it was made by professional gambler Dennis O'Kelly who was betting on his prediction when the great racehorse appeared in public for the first time, in 1769, and duly landed O'Kelly's bet, winning by a furlong, with his opponents too far behind to be officially placed.

Jockey George Fordham had ridden a horse in such a way as to displease its notoriously awkward owner, Lady Lindsay, who told him, 'You can hand in my colours, Fordham. You will never ride for me again.' Fordham replied, 'Will your grace stay where she is for a few seconds, till I get her colours from the weighing-room? I'd like your grace to have them now, lest your grace changes her mind.'

Bernard van Cutsem was asked by the press, following a winner in a race at Royal Ascot, 'What are your plans

'Eclipse first, the rest nowhere . . .'

for this horse?'

'Dear boy,' he replied, 'That *was* the plan.'

A trainer, who must remain nameless, gave his opinion of owners to a fellow trainer: 'Treat them like mushrooms - keep them in the dark as long as you can, well filled up with manure.'

1950s bandleader Maurice Winnick was a presenter of the *What's My Line?* TV programme - he was also a keen punter who once asked a bookie for a £400 bet, but was told the bookie would only accept £40. Winnick told the bookie who he was and asked him if he'd like to appear on What's My Line. When he replied that he would Winnick said, 'You'll do well, nobody would ever guess you're a bloody bookmaker.'

How They See Racing 1: Charles Greville, a famous diarist, and owner of 1837 St Leger winner Mango, wrote in 1838, 'Racing is just like dram drinking; momentary excitement and wretched intervals; full consciousness of the mischievous effects of the habit and equal difficulty in abstaining from it.'

How They See Racing 2: Actor Paul Eddington, well known for his role as Jim Hacker in TV's *Yes, Minister*, was once asked his opinion of horseracing and duly obliged: 'It bores me. The attraction must be something to do with sex - lavish preparation, sudden ejaculation, followed by a lengthy period of regret.'

RACING MEDIA

The first person to attempt to catalogue the results of horse races in the UK was John Cheny of Arundel in 1726.

Fifty years ago, before satellite communications and cellular telephones, the work of the news agency reporters at the race course called for the kinds of skill more generally associated with Boy Scouts than journalists! A typical team of reporters consisted of three men. One inside the course, one with binoculars or a telescope outside the course, and the third man up a telegraph pole, tapping, with Post Office approval, into a telephone line. The man on the course signalled the odds and results by tic-tac, which was read by the man with telescope, who shouted the information to the man on the wire. Needless to say, everything did not always go to plan, the occasional reporter having to be plucked from a muddy ditch! However, even that cumbersome system was easy compared to what was necessary at some courses. At Goodwood, carrier pigeons were employed because the Duke forbade telegraph poles on his land. And at an Irish course on the coast, surrounded by hills, the telescope man had to operate from a boat and pass on the signals to the telephonist on the other side of a hill.

These and other fascinating facts about the early days of the sporting news service, are described in *Extel 100: The Centenary History of the Exchange Telegraph Company* by JM Scott (Benn 1972).

There was great interest throughout the land about the outcome of big races in the early nineteenth century, but there was a problem in spreading the news of who had won. Until 1825, when Memnon's St Leger victory became the first result to be carried by a pigeon, from Doncaster to London.

Jockeys have to get used to criticism, but G Barclay got really upset in 1936 when the *Evening Star* newspaper in New Zealand criticised his riding – he sued for £500 damages. The judge dismissed Barclay's claim, saying, 'Jockeys must expect criticism, so long as the facts are truly stated and comment does not convey imputations of an evil sort.'

Probably the first race meeting to receive detailed radio coverage was the Canterbury Jockey Club meeting

'I'm just being handed a late racing result . . .'

in New Zealand in November 1926 – although considering that there were only reckoned to be 2000 radio sets in the country at that time the audience was somewhat limited. The first commentaries were broadcast from the top of a haystack near the start because local officials did not want to distract patrons in the stand. The Aintree Grand National was not broadcast until 1927.

TIPSTERS

Bob Butchers – Newsboy of the *Daily Mirror* – could justifiably claim to be the most successful tipster ever. In a career running from December 1946 to April 1985 he tipped well over 43,000 winners for *Mirror* readers.

Followers of *Morning Star* tipster Cayton (Alf Rubin) cheered long and loud as his Nap selection for October 4, 1986 stormed home at odds of 4-9 in a three-horse field. Cayton was ending a record run of losers, having previously tipped 57 consecutive losing Naps.

Sun newspaper tipster Claud 'The Punters' Pal' Duval was rash enough to promise to walk nude around Portman Square, which contains the HQ of the Jockey Club, if that august body did not reinstate Royal Gait, who had been disqualified as the winner of the 1988 Ascot Gold Cup. The Jockey Club declined to reinstate

the horse and following my call to Kelvin McKenzie, Editor of *The Sun*, to remind him of his racing correspondent's pledge, Claud duly lost his shirt and the rest of his clothes in London W1.

Chris Hawkins of *The Guardian* has been 'through the card' 15 times. Marten Julian, who digs out likely winners for readers of his *Dark Horse Annual* has a degree in theology - does he have the benefit of divine inspiration?

Star-struck punters searching for information were able to dial up tips from Teri King's Star Line in 1989. Teri, an astrologer, cast the horsocopes of top trainers and jockeys and then forecast which of them would be lucky. Judging by the rambling, inconclusive nature of the 'tips', I would say that Teri herself was likely to be the biggest winner, coining in the revenue from calls charged at up to 38p per minute.

A £20 winning bet on 3-1 chance Diplomatic Bag in the late fifties financed the honeymoon of racing journalist Charles Benson. Had the horse lost, the penniless Benson would probably have been heading straight for the divorce courts.

BBC World Service racing commentator Christopher Poole is patiently waiting for the running of his dream Derby. In June 1989 he revealed, 'Four years ago, prone in a hospital bed and wondering whether it was worthwhile recovering from a multiple heart bypass operation, I "watched" a Derby being run in vivid colour complete with stereophonic sound.' In Poole's dream the Derby winner is trained by Richard Hannon, ridden by Brian Rouse, is a grey colt and wins by two lengths at odds of 25-1 on a sunny afternoon with fast going. 'My assurance that the dream formula will come true one Derby day remains unshakeable as does the belief that it will happen in time for me to retain enough verve for the millionaires' playgrounds,' declares the 51-year-old Poole.

TV commentator Derek Thompson feared he might be on his way to the Tower after beating Prince Charles at Plumpton. The heir to the throne finished second on Long Wharf on his first ride in public in March 1980. Thompson rode Classified.

TV executive Michael Grade, currently top man at Channel 4, worked on the racing desk at the *Daily Mirror* in the early days of his career when, he confesses, his knowledge of the sport was somewhat basic, as is revealed by the anecdote he tells against himself concerning an interview he carried out with legendary trainer Vincent O'Brien. Grade had begun the interview by asking O'Brien 'What's been your most thrilling moment in racing so far?' to which he replied, 'I think it was when I won the Oaks with a filly called . . .' At which point the over-enthusiastic Grade butted in with 'You mean you won the Oaks with a filly?'

A couple of the least likely racing stories to appear for some years were reported by the *Sunday Sport* during 1989. First they 'revealed' that

kidnapped racehorse Shergar had been seen on Dartmoor, being ridden by Lord Lucan. Then they followed that story with another, apparently penned by their racing correspondent Derek Thompson, that Lucan had been spotted enjoying a day at the races.

Not quite the Holy Grail, but very highly prized amongst collectors of racing memorabilia is the book *The Best Horses Of 1942*, written by one William K Temple, which is in fact the pseudonym used by the late Phil Bull, founder of the Timeform racing information service. The 1942 publication, the forerunner of today's annual *Racehorses Of 1989, 1990* etc, changes hands for up to £1000, equalled in equine literary circles only by the autobiography of American jockey Tod Sloan who first introduced the 'monkey up a stick'

style of riding to Britain (see page 61).

Racing professionals were at a loss to understand just what they might be letting themselves in for when they received a letter from France inviting them to advertise in or subscribe to a new racing publication. Said the letter, distributed in January 1989, 'Dear Mrs, Dear Mr. We are very pleased to inform you of the parution in January 1989 of the Horses Directory. Informative and advertising year book, it is a most experted event in turf circle. As soon as published, this work had vocation to propose to the Races World all the informations about the bloodstocks' career, and professionals activities during the last year. That's why its diffusion and notoriety don't stop increasing.'

It hardly set the charts alight, but the 1979 single on the Pye label, 'Red Rum's Song' by Christopher, Robin, Alice & Ted featured commentator Peter Bromley's dulcet tones taken from his BBC report on the Grand National.

Some famous horseracing films:

Champions - the story of Bob Champion and Aldaniti's Grand National triumph, starring John Hurt.

National Velvet - Elizabeth Taylor wins the Grand National.

A Day At The Races - racecourse mayhem with the Marx Brothers.

Rainbow Jacket - the film which inspired Willie Carson's ambition to become a jockey.

COURSES FOR HORSES

Chester is believed to have been the first course to stage organised public racing in the UK, with races taking place from early in the sixteenth century.

Doncaster may have been the first racecourse to boast a groundsman - in 1614 according to old corporation records, Anthony Hogg was paid one shilling and sixpence for 'making the waye at the horse race'.

In 1706 Stirling racecourse in Scotland offered its patrons not only horse racing and foot racing during its programme, but also goose racing.

In 1780 Edinburgh advocate Hugo Arnot wrote a history of his city and included details about the local race meeting, 'commonly held in the summer season over the sands at Leith, which are heavy and fatiguing for the horses, especially if they are not of strong bottom. The races last for a week. The prizes run for are: a piece of plate of 50 guineas given by the City of Edinburgh; a purse of 50 guineas given by Sir Lawrence Dundas, the City's representative in Parliament; another purse for 50 guineas by subscription of the nobility and gentry to be run for by actual hunters; His Majesty's purse of 100 guineas; the Ladies' subscription purse and the noble and gentlemen's purse of 100 guineas.'

Racing is believed to have begun in Ireland in 1686 with a meeting at the Curragh of Kildare.

The first race meeting held at Melbourne, Australia, took place in March 1838 - there were two races, bullock trucks served as the grandstand, a clothes prop was the winning post and bets were struck and settled in bottles of rum.

In 1898 the *Sportsman* newspaper carried details of the day's racing at Trodmore racecourse. Trodmore did not, however, exist. The meeting had been set up so that a band of rogue punters could place bets and then supply the paper with their own results, which they duly did. By the time anyone became suspicious, the punters had been paid out and no trace could be found of the man who had supplied the *Sportsman* with the Trodmore runners and results.

They've been racing at Ireland's Laytown course since 1876 - but they're still not exactly sure where the track is. For Laytown is actually a course on a beach and only when the tide goes out on the morning of the meeting is it decided exactly where the course will be placed this year. Once a jockey had to be rescued from drowning during a race - Nicky Brennan's mount took off with him and galloped into the Irish Sea, not remotely interested to learn that Brennan couldn't swim a stroke. He was eventually saved.

English traders settled in Japan in the mid-nineteenth century and soon created a racecourse at Yokohama, holding the first race meeting there in May 1862. However, a meeting taking place in August faced problems unheard of at Ascot or Newmarket when, apparently offended by the new sport, Samurai warriors attacked and killed a number of English jockeys competing in a race.

The Blaydon Races, subject of the song, last took place in 1916.

Possibly the most famous racing picture of all time is 'The Derby Day', painted in 1858 by William Powell Frith (1819-1909), although it has to be admitted the artist dwells more on the motley crowd of racegoers than on the thoroughbreds! Frith's first experience of the races was a visit to the long-disappeared course at Hampton in Middlesex. In his autobiography he reveals how he watched with fascinated horror while an unsuccessful racegoer tried to cut his own throat! This and other incidents suggested to Frith that here was a subject for an interesting painting. Frith's lady companion was not impressed with the idea but, fortunately for art lovers, the artist was not discouraged. Using the Epsom Derby as his setting, he went to create one of the greatest masterpieces of narrative art. The original hangs in the Tate Gallery, London.

In 1935 veteran English actor Wilfred Hyde White visited Ascot racecourse just before the Royal meeting, only to experience the apparition of a meeting taking place. Hyde White said that a voice began to announce runners and riders – a system then not even invented – and that while he and a friend listened, the names of the winners of all the races on the card were announced. Hyde White, a keen follower of the Turf, didn't recognise the names of any of the phantom runners and henceforward kept waiting eagerly for the meeting to take place.

When Hollywood Park racecourse opened in 1938 shareholders included Walt Disney, Sam Goldwyn and Bing Crosby. The course also boasts the Cary Grant Pavilion.

Longchamp racecourse in France was the first to use sex to attract racegoers to the track. John Cobb, writing in *The Independent* in February 1989, reported, 'An advertisement broadcast on television would have many a Jockey Club member dropping his monocle in a state of shock. In the advert, a scantily dressed girl lies on a bed and pouts to her male companion, "Why don't we have fun any more?" "You want action?" he replies and moves closer. The strap from her slip starts to drop away . . . and then cut to the stalls bursting open at Longchamp and the same couple leaping up and down as they cheer a winner home.'

Fans of radio's most popular soap opera, *The Archers*, should avoid the nearby racecourse, if an edition of the series' local paper, *The Borchester Echo*, is anything to go by. A recent edition, produced for Archers' followers, listed details of 'Saturday's card at Felpersham'. It sounds like a remarkable meeting, with a three mile race on the Flat in which two of the runners fell in recent outings and one unseated its rider; a six furlong race in which only five of the seven runners will start from the stalls; and a mile race in which one of the runners boasts the interesting form figures – FFOOZF!

Newton Abbot racecourse witnessed a bizarre ceremony when the ashes of racing fan and punter Alan Rix were scattered over the course in May 1989. 62-year-old Alan of Cornwall had no relatives so when he died Mrs Patti Wong, owner of his local Chinese restaurant, paid for his funeral, filled his coffin with betting slips and a copy of the *Sporting Life* and then organised the ceremony at the racetrack. 'Chinese people believe you should take some of your living things with you when you die,' explained Mrs Wong.

The entire Tote system at Huntingdon racecourse was scuppered in November 1988 when rats chewed through a main cable.

America's Saratoga track has become known as 'the graveyard for favourites'. Champions Man O' War, Gallant Fox and Secretariat were all beaten here – and legendary gambler John 'Bet A Million' Gates once lost $400,000 at one meeting.

The following racecourses have closed since 1960:

Course	*Last meeting*
Buckfastleigh	Aug 27, 1960
Hurst Park	Oct 10, 1962
Woore	June 1, 1963
Manchester	Nov 9, 1963
Lincoln	May 21, 1964
Lewes	Sept 14, 1964
Bogside	Apr 10, 1965
Rothbury	Apr 10, 1965
Birmingham	June 21, 1965
Alexandra Park	Sept 8, 1970
Wye	May 2, 1974
Lanark	Oct 18, 1977
Stockton	June 16, 1981

Mark Qualey and Johna McCutcheon were married in the winners enclosure at Gulfstream Park, Florida immediately after the running of the Herecomesthebride Stakes in April, 1987.

When Sam Baxter of Cambridgeshire died in 1986, his ashes were scattered by the winning post of his favourite racecourse, Huntingdon.

Stratford racecourse is 'twinned' with Ovrevoll racecourse in Norway.

Jockeys racing at Delta Downs racecourse, Louisiana, sometimes feel the urge to make it snappy - because there are two infield ponds at the track which are home to a number of alligators! Course spokesman Steve Nick told me, 'Two years ago one summer, one of them decided to take in the sun rays on the track - and spent most of the day on the turn leading towards the stretch.' Fortunately there were no old 'crocks' racing that day and no-one was hurt.

At St Moritz in Switzerland they hold a race meeting on the local lake when it is iced over during the winter. The runners wear studded horseshoes and gallop round the tight six-furlong circuit.

Canadian writer Don Dunn tells of an incident at Landsdowne Races in Vancouver. 'Landsdowne's surface, particularly in front of the grandstand, has a little more substance to it. The septic tank emptied into a ditch on the inside rail. This ditch was periodically dredged and added to the track's surface. One day a horse pulled up and dumped his rider just past the wire. The Italian-American jockey fell off face first. He jumped up, exclaiming, "This stuff not only looka like s**t - it tasta like s**t!" '

Dunn also recalls another occasion at Landsdowne in the days before photo-finishes when a horse called Princess Sally 'ran down the track on the outside fence. She won, but the stewards did not see her and placed the horses on the inside 1–2–3. The order was made official and Princess Sally was not in the money.'

The Airdrie and Coatbridge local paper was not exactly one of the greatest fans of the 1861 race meeting held at Airdrie - saying it brought only 'fast youths, fancy men, gamblers, blacklegs and women of easy virtue' to the area.

Racing at the Hippodrome, Notting Hill, London. From an old wood engraving. (Courtesy: David Bennett)

The sporting scene in pleasant country surroundings shown in the above engraving is not a scene you would normally associate with the bustling area of Notting Hill, London! How this course came about and why it did not survive are given in the following account from about 1850:

'As a new feature in the racing world, an attempt was made to establish race meetings, and also a training locality, within two miles of the metropolis. To this extent a large portion of land was treated for and engaged close to Notting Hill. Here stabling and boxes for about seventy-five racehorses were erected, with every convenience for a training establishment; a very good racecourse formed, and numerous stakes were run for on it in 1838. But unfortunately, the projectors overlooked one circumstance at once fatal to the Hippodrome (as the establishment was named); the soil was a deep strong clay, so that the training ground could only be gone on by horses at particular periods. This was a difficulty not to be got over, and, as a racecourse, the Hippodrome closed its short career, doubtless with heavy loss to its projectors.'

What might have been!

GIRL RACERS

FIRST LADIES

Lady jockeys are still not completely accepted these days - but perhaps the first lady jockey to ride a winner was noted some three hundred years ago by the *Chester Recorder*, whose diary for March 7 1691 noted, 'We rode to Farne race where I run against Sir Edmund Ashton, Mrs Morte, Mr Mackworth and Captain Warburton. Mrs Morte won the race.'

Lady Nelson became the first of her sex to own an Aintree winner over fences when Ally Sloper won the Stanley Steeplechase in 1914. The following year saw Ally Sloper win the Grand National, making Lady Nelson the first woman to a own a Grand National winner.

Mrs Anne Ferris was the first lady to ride the winner of the Irish Grand National when she and 33-1 shot Bentom Boy came home in 1984. No lady has won the Aintree version, but Charlotte Brew was the first to try, on Barony Fort in 1977 and Geraldine Rees the first to get round, on Cheers in 1982, a year before Jenny Pitman became the first lady to train the winner - Corbiere.

The first lady to ride six winners in a day was Julie Krone of the US who did it at Aqueduct, New York.

The first woman to ride a Derby winner was Linda Jones who won the New Zealand equivalent in the late seventies.

The first woman professional jockey in France was Caroline Lee. Born in Dublin in 1963, she went to France in 1980 and has already clocked up over 125 winners. In 1988 she was the first lady to ride in the French Derby, finishing 10th on Face Nord.

Gay Kelleway was the first lady to win at Royal Ascot, on Sprowston Boy in the Queen Alexandra Stakes.

Helen Johnson Houghton was the first lady to train an English Classic winner - Gilles de Retz, 2000 Guineas winner in 1956. At the time ladies were not officially recognised as trainers.

Meriel Tufnell was the first winner of a Ladies' race, riding Scorched Earth at Kempton in 1972.

First woman to officially train a winner in Great Britain over the jumps was Jackie Brutton when Snowdra Queen won at Cheltenham on March 16, 1966. Flat counterpart was Norah Wilmot with Pat at Brighton on August 3, 1966.

Morag Chalmers took over from David McHarg at Hamilton in August 1988 to become the first female Clerk of the Course.

Princess Anne became the first lady Royal to ride a winner - Gulfland at Redcar in 1982.

Gee Armytage rode Gee-A to become the first lady to ride a winner at the Cheltenham Festival in 1987.

Caroline Beasley was the first female to win over the Aintree fences - on Eliogarty in the 1986 Foxhunters Chase.

Lady Meux was the first lady to breed a Classic winner - Volodyovski, the 1901 Derby winner.

Lady James Douglas became the first woman to own a Derby winner when her Gainsborough won in 1918.

Mrs Charmian Hill, later to own Dawn Run, became the first lady rider to compete against men in Ireland when she finished third in a National Hunt flat race at Fairyhouse in January 1973.

Janet Slade was the first lady jockey to ride a winner over fences in France, in 1973.

In 1966 Norah Wilmot became the first official woman trainer.

In 1937 Mrs GBMiller became the first woman to own the winner of the Epsom Derby. Judging by a report in the *Daily Sketch* newspaper, she was less than overwhelmed by the achievement. 'I've been photographed a thousand times,' she told a reporter, 'and really, it's an awful fuss.' The *Daily Sketch* reporter pointed out that it was a national event and millions of people were celebrating. 'Celebrate?' she said. 'Does one celebrate? We are having dinner in the ordinary way.' Her horse, Mid Day Sun, was a 100–7 chance.

Elwood struck a blow for women's lib by becoming the first horse owned by a woman to run in the Kentucky Derby. Mrs Charles Durnell's colt won the 1904 running, when he was also the first winner bred by a woman, Mrs J Prather.

Women jockeys have had to fight to be accepted on equal terms - but not always as literally as American girl Julie Krone. In 1986 Julie, with over 1200 winners to her credit, had something of a contretemps during a race at the Monmouth track. Miguel

Rujano, trying to find some extra space, asked her to move over by lashing her across the face with his whip. Whilst the pair were waiting to weigh in after the race, Julie cracked him with a right hook to the jaw, following up with a chair over the head when the two met again later near a local swimming pool.

They were both fined $100 - but you can be sure that no one messes with Julie anymore.

Jockey Gee Armytage broke her collarbone in a fall. While she was being examined by physio John Skull, her boyfriend Carl Llewellyn was waiting outside the surgery. As Gee's shoulder was being manipulated she cried out in pain several times - which so affected the waiting Llewellyn that he began to feel faint and then actually collapsed.

Severe asthma attacks forced Pamela Rouse, daughter of jockey Brian Rouse, to give up riding, despite being good enough to compete at Royal Ascot. Her choice of a new career was slightly surprising - topless modelling. She launched it by appearing more out of than in a set of jockey silks in *The People* newspaper on June 25 1989. 'I have always had a secret ambition to be a Page Three girl,' she was reported as saying. 'I don't think my Dad really approves.' Still, perhaps there is still time for her to make a mark as a jockey. After all, Dad Brian rode his first winner in 1957 and his second in 1972.

American female jockey Robyn Smith used to own a mink covered saddle.

Race followers visiting the Harrods winter sale during 1987 were surprised to be served by lady jockey Maxine Juster.

Lester Piggott's daughter Tracy can boast a better riding record than her famous Dad's - hers is a 100 per cent record - one ride, one win.

Annabel King, who trains at Stratford-upon-Avon, is known as 'The Lady In Red' because of her habit of always wearing that colour.

The world's only race exclusively for Nuns takes place at Trim, Ireland. In 1988 the first running of the race was won by Sister Anne riding Sweet Divine, and in 1989 local Nun Sister Olive Irwin came home first on 10–1 chance Bright Star, beating seven opponents and winning a first prize of £1000 to donate to the charity of her choice.

The finishing touches to the Cheltenham Festival preparations of She's Pretty in 1989 were carried out by 53-year-old Irish Nun Sister Patrick of Navan, County Meath, who exercised the five-year-old hurdler on the sands at Laytown. Sister Patrick said, 'We are allowed to use our little bit of pocket money as we wish. I often have a little flutter. My biggest bet was £1 each way and I won at 7–1.'

RACING ROYALS

In 1389 France's King Charles VI and his brother, the Duc de Touraine, raced from Montpelier to Paris for 5000 francs. The Duc took four days and a third, the King four and a half.

Preparing for a challenge horse race in France in 1517, the Duke of Suffolk is said to have given his horse no hay for three days and restricted his own diet to white wine for the same period. Perhaps not too surprisingly, the Duke was beaten.

King James I once enjoyed a day's racing at Hereford where the people responsible for the sport decided to add to the day's attractions with a display of Morris Dancing by ten local chaps - whose combined ages, according to contemporary reports, added up to over a thousand.

Charles II, the 'Merry Monarch', is the only reigning King to have ridden a winner - he won the 1671 Newmarket Town Plate.

She may or may not have said 'Let them eat cake', but Marie Antoinette was certainly a keen racegoer. A contemporary report noted, 'Every week there are several horse races and the Queen, who has acquired an extraordinary taste for this kind of spectacle, has not missed one.'

Ascot racecourse witnessed one of the oddest events in its lengthy history in the late eighteenth century when King George IV, who as Prince Regent won the 1788 Derby with Sir Thomas, was assaulted by a one-legged former sailor who lobbed a stone at the Royal personage, damaging his hat. The mischievious matelot, one Dennis Collins, who had apparently only just acquired a new wooden limb in order to attend the races, was brought to justice and given what might seem to be a somewhat harsh penalty - he was sentenced to be hung, drawn and quartered. He eventually got away with transportation and lasted a good while before dying in exile. The King, too, soon scaled down his racing activities, following a scandal over the running of one of his horses, even though his own integrity was not questioned.

Queen Victoria was distinctly unamused by her son the Prince of Wales' love of racing - so much so that in 1867 she wrote to him, saying, 'Dearest Bertie, Now that Ascot races are approaching, I wish to repeat earnestly and seriously that I trust you will confine your visits to the Races to two days . . . your example can do much for good and do a great

deal for evil.' The Prince, then aged 28, rejected her request.

A special race meeting was organised in 1821, however, at the Curragh, Ireland, for the newly-crowned King George IV. Special toilet facilities were erected at the course - with an exceptionally large seat to accomodate the Royal person.

King Edward VII, an enthusiastic owner, died on May 6, 1910. It is said that the last piece of information relayed to him on his death bed concerned the success of one of his horses in a race at Kempton.

We know he used to enjoy the occasional outing under rules as a jockey, but Prince Charles may not be quite so successful as a punter. During his 1985 tour of Australia, the Prince presented the trophy for that country's top race, the Melbourne Cup, to winning jockey Pat Hyland, telling him, 'I will excuse the fact that you beat the horse I put my money on by a very short head.'

Although her personal Press Officer, Major A Griffin, told me in 1986 that the Queen Mother does not bet and 'to the best of my knowledge never has done', *Today* newspaper reported in April 1989 that Her Majesty had ordered a satellite dish for her Clarence House home 'so she can follow her runners on racecourses throughout the realm via the latest high-tech system, SIS (Satellite Information Services). The gambling great-grandmother has until now made do with the Extel tannoy system,' it revealed. The paper also quoted a recent guest of Her Majesty as saying that the Queen Mother had disappeared during tea for a few minutes. 'The sound of racing commentators gave the game away and when she returned, Her Majesty had that special glow of a winner.'

British Empire Decorations for public service have gone to the following racing personalities:

OBE:
Lester Piggott (Annulled in June 1988)
Lord Oaksey
Willie Carson
Joe Mercer
Peter O'Sullevan

MBE:
Bob Champion

CBE:
Fred Winter

COMMANDER OF THE VICTORIAN ORDER (Given as personal gift by the Queen)
Royal Trainers
Fulke Walwyn
Dick Hern

YOU BET!

INSIDER GAMBLING

Several months before the 1871 National, Lord Poulett, owner of The Lamb, wrote to jockey Tommy Pickernell. 'I dreamt twice last night I saw the race run. The first dream he was last. The second dream, I should think an hour afterwards, I saw the Liverpool run. He won by four lengths and you rode him.' Poulett plunged fortunes on the horse who, ridden by Pickernell, won at odds of 5–1 by two lengths.

Jockey Richard Goodisson, who rode the winners of the first three runnings of the Oaks in 1779, '80 and '81 was reputed always to carry £500 in cash about his person following the occasion on which he had been refused a credit bet of that amount – which duly won.

Trainer Tom Dawson won £25,000 in bets when Ellington won the 1856

Derby. He put it all in a silk hat box which he then managed to leave on a train. The hat box was returned to him a week later, having been handed in after travelling to Edinburgh, Aberdeen and Yorkshire - every penny was still there.

Desperate to prevent anyone else discovering what was going on when a horse was being especially prepared to land a gamble, betting trainer Atty Persse would lock his stable lads into their sleeping quarters every night for fear that they might spill the beans.

Geoffrey Hamlyn has worked on racecourses since 1928 and whilst carrying out his job of returning the official starting price of horses he witnessed many notable gambles. 'One which stands out in my mind was in 1933 and it must be one of the most extraordinary in the history of the Derby. Miss Dorothy Paget had a horse running called Tuppence who was rightly priced up at 100–1. Twenty minutes or so before the 'off' there was a message to invest £2000 on the horse - the equivalent of about £100,000 today - and agents went flying in all directions. They had a bit at 100–1, a couple of hundred or so at 50–1 and 33s and most of the remainder at all prices down to and including 10–1. Tuppence finished 19th of 26. It was obviously Miss Paget's money. She was not renowned for her sagacity.'

Jamaican businessman Robert de Lisser put £40,000 on his horse Pactolus to win the 1986 Cesarewitch - to try to win enough to pay his wife Nina's alimony as a result of their divorce. The horse finished out of the first dozen.

The exact amount seemed to be slightly in doubt but owner Tony Gleeson, a publican from Ealing, certainly cleaned up when his Rotherfield Greys won the 1988 William Hill Stewards Cup. 'My winnings come to £250,000 while the family as a whole must be due at least £500,000' he told the *Sporting Life*, while *The Sun* reported him as saying, 'With all my family and pals, we walked off a million quid richer.'

It was a case of 'heads you lose, tails we win' at Oakley point-to-point meeting in Northamptonshire in June, 1989 where, following a dead heat for first place in one race the Tote returned stakes to those who had backed either winner - and kept the rest of the pool.

Sydney racehorse-owner Colin Tidy gave his 16-year-old son Robert £40 to take his friends out for a meal. After they'd eaten they found they still had some change, so they went along to the local Rosehill racecourse where they won over £100,000 backing six winners on the trot including his Dad's horse, Zeditave. His Dad said later, 'Robert shouldn't have been betting. I've banned him from going to the races again until he's 18.'

Very few 200–1 shots win races - still fewer carry anyone's money. In January 1989, Allerlad was a shock 100–1 winner at Ayr. It was certainly a shock for his owner-trainer David

McDonald, who didn't have a penny on the horse. But form-studying journalist Alan Amies had shrewdly placed a bet of £20 each way on the horse when it was being quoted on the course at odds of 200–1. 'The whole of Ayr could hear me shouting him home,' he said as he collected his £4800 winnings.

Not even Alan Amies fancied the chances of Park Slave in a novice hurdle race at Wetherby in January 1988. He was quoted at 3000–1, probably the longest odds seen on a British racetrack, and finished 7th.

En route to Doncaster races, former champion jump jockey John Francome was asked by a buffet attendant if he could tip him a horse. Francome suggested a 20–1 outsider which duly obliged. Having forgotten all about the incident Francome was a little surprised several weeks later to be greeted like a long lost brother by the same delighted attendant, telling him what a wonderful chap he was. Francome asked him if he'd backed the horse, to be told that the attendant had plunged most of his savings - £300 - on the horse and won £6000.

Just like anglers are always telling stories of 'the one that got away', so every punter can tell the tale of the day he nearly cleaned up. But few of them can compete with Terry Ramsden's almost-but-not-quite yarn. In August 1986 the owner and fearless backer, who made a fortune operating in the Japanese financial markets, staked a £10,000 win treble on three runners trained by Alan Bailey. Lack A Style won at Newmarket at 16–1, giving him £170,000 going on to Cry For The Clown, who won at 4–1. Ramsden now stood to win a mere £8.5 million if his final selection, 9–1 shot Miss Milveagh, obliged. The filly led into the final furlong but was caught and beaten close home by Remain Free, and Ramsden missed out on a huge pay-out.

Peter O'Sullevan once told how his best ever win was on a horse called Indian Queen which he backed at 50–1 in the 1950s after receiving a tip from a trainer. He then had to deliver a calm commentary as the horse raced home, landing him a win of £2500. In an interview with *The Sun*, O'Sullevan estimated that he bets on average £20,000 a year.

Former jockey, TV commentator and journalist, John Oaksey revealed that a point-to-point meeting gave him the taste for enjoying a flutter. Not only did he ride his first winner there in 1951, but 'The Pegasus Club was responsible for another life-long addiction, because it was there that I backed my first winner.' Still at school, Oaksey risked ten bob (50p) on the nose of a 20–1 shot trained by his sister - an 18-year-old hunter, Lohengrin, ridden by 'a genial law student called Gerald Ponsonby who freely admitted that his fitness left a lot to be desired, but since he was just there to make up the numbers nobody thought it would matter.'

Lohengrin duly set off at the rear of the field and stayed there until his rivals, one by one, came to grief, leaving him clear at the second last, at which point the tiring Gerald was unseated. He was helped back into the saddle but a remounted rival was beginning to make ground. Lohengrin dislodged Gerald again. 'The lone pursuer was closing fast. Both Lohengrin and Gerald were exhausted and my ten bob looked in deadly danger after all. But all was well. A huge farmer threw Gerald back aboard and without stirrups, whip or hat, he rode for home like a hero. Three quarters of a rapidly disappearing length was the verdict in the end - and of all the great finishes I have seen since, nothing, not even Crisp and Red Rum or Special Cargo's Whitbread, has meant more to me at the time.'

PUNTERS

Three punters grabbed a share of the world record dividend for a single bet, paid out in Hong Kong in March 1989. One punter staked 90p, one staked £1.80 and a third £12,575 to win a slice of the £2.4 million payout from the Double Trio bet which requires punters to predict the first three home in two selected races.

In 1947 when jockey Gordon Richards was at the height of his powers, a punter thought he'd come up with a surefire way of making his betting pay. He made a standing order bet with his bookmaker that he wanted to back Gordon's best mount of the day to win him £1000. All went well, with many more winners than losers until one fateful day in June when Gordon rode 20-1 ON shot Glendower in a two horse race, which meant the punter was investing £20,000 to win £1000. Glendower whipped round at the start of the race and unseated Gordon, leaving his solitary opponent Markwell to win as he liked.

Steve Saunders used up all his courage in placing a £5000 bet on a horse called Astral at Plumpton. Then minutes before the off, Steve, convinced he was going to lose his money, threw his betting slip away. Astral duly romped home at 4-6, and Steve's bookie refused to pay out without the original betting slip - so part-time grave-digger Steve had to organise his friends to search the gutters of Wimborne, Dorset for the ticket, which turned up several hours later.

All punters have their hard luck stories - but Mel Foster felt particularly aggrieved when Nagwa let him down when he had six winners in a seven selection bet - he stood to win £9000, and the horse went on to win sixteen races that season.

Chinese chef Tony Tang took away £217,708 from a Catford betting shop after backing four winners for a £100 stake in 1988.

Aldershot businessman George Rhodes landed world record odds of 1,670,759-1 when he collected £86,056.42 for a 5p seven horse accumulator. He thought he'd use his winnings 'to buy another Rolls'.

Edward Hodson of Wolverhampton thought he was made for life in 1984 when his 5p yankee bet produced four winners at combined odds of 3,956,748-1 - sadly for Edward he soon found out that his bookie's maximum payout was £3000.

The biggest single betting shop cash bet recorded occurred on Derby Day, 1985, when a punter strolled into a Park Lane shop and told staff 'I'd like to make a little bet on Shadeed, please.' He pulled out bundles of £50 notes and staked £50,000 cash on the 5-2 shot, which was beaten.

Stuart Starr and William Allen laid out $48 and scooped $600,000 by landing the Pick Nine Pool at Calder racecourse, Miami, in October 1986.

Paul Cooper picked up a cool £250,000 with a tricast bet placed at a betting shop in Lower Richmond Road in May 1989. Cooper laid out £16.50 and Miss Daisy (20–1), Halvoya (25–1) and Roysia Boy (33–1) duly came in 1st, 2nd and 3rd in the Dick Peacock Handicap at Thirsk to make him a rich man.

On the same day, a 26-year-old man from Dartford, London picked out five horses whose name began with the letter M, as a tribute to his recently deceased sister whose name also began with M. For his £3.10 bet he won £22,900 from William Hill as Miss Daisy (20–1), My Lamb (9–1), Make Or Mar (5–1), Midfielder (12–1) and Must Be Magic (14–1) won.

With the middle name Arkle, Tom Urquhart just had to be interested in horses, and by the age of thirteen the youngster was already exciting much comment with his winner finding ability. The *Sunday Express*, in March 1989, told how Tom, a pupil at the Roman Catholic boarding school Belmont Abbey, in Herefordshire, run by monks, tipped nine winners out of a possible 18 at the 1988 Cheltenham

Festival and found a further six in 1989. Tom's father, aware of his son's talent, drove to the school to smuggle in a copy of the *Sporting Life* and his boy promptly obliged with three winners at odds of 20–1, 4–1 and 7–2. 'Sensing an opportunity for early retirement,' reported the *Express*, 'Mr Urquhart returned to Belmont Abbey the following morning with that day's edition of the *'Life*, only to be intercepted by one of the monks who told him, "I'd like a word with you in my study." Trembling with apprehension, Mr Urquhart said he was sorry, it was only a bit of fun and it wouldn't happen again . . . "Don't worry about it," soothed this man of God, "Just next time you get the tips like that, make sure he gives them to us as well!"'

Professional punter Helmut Flann of Austria claims to make £150,000 a year out of his activites – with the help of the ghost of his deceased Aunt Sally. And he even went to court to fight for the custody of the ghost when his ex-wife started to make claims on him. 'I earn something like £150,000 a year at horse tracks throughout Europe and a lot of my best tips come from Aunt Sally. By actively encouraging my dear dead Aunt to stay with her, my ex-wife is trying to deprive me of her company and my livelihood.'

Four Indonesians who had inherited an estimated £80 million fortune came and spent £2.6 million of it in one London betting shop between April 24 and June 26 1987.

In the mid-1800s bookmaker William Davies, known as The Leviathan, would take bets of up to £50,000 on a horse.

Within the space of an hour and three quarters one punter laid out £205,000 in bets at York's 1989 August meeting – and at the end of the hour and three quarters all he had to show for it was . . . £205,000. He started off in the 3.10 race by losing £90,000 on beaten 4–9 chance Cacoethes. Thirty-five minutes later he plunged £25,000 on Zalazl at 2–1 which duly obliged then at 4.45 out came another £90,000 to go on Weld at 4–9, which got home by a mere neck.

Emilio Scala was £354,544 better off following Grakle's 1931 Grand National victory. He didn't ride, own or train the horse, but he bought the winning 50p ticket in the first Irish Hospital Sweepstakes.

Richard Goodfellow volunteered to do his good deed for the day by placing a 1989 Derby day bet for his next door neighbour, Dave Heaton. But when Richard reached the William Hill shop in Preston he was struck by a bout of amnesia. He knew the horse which Dave wanted to put a fiver each way on began with 'T' – but was it Torjoun or Terimon? Richard plumped for Terimon and got an awful telling off from Dave, who knew that Terimon was a 500–1 no-hoper while Torjoun was a well fancied 11–1: 'When he told me he'd put it on the wrong horse, I could have killed him.' But not for long – for no-hoper Terimon romped into second place at 500–1 and won £500 for delighted Dave, who soon changed his tune: 'I could have kissed him.'

Adrian Booth made his selection for the 1992 Derby on May 18, 1989 – at which time the horse he backed was less than two days old and didn't even have a name!

Adrian, from Northampton, read an article in the *Racing Post* which said that Sun Princess had produced a bay colt by Rainbow Quest, born at the Ballymacoll Stud, Meath at five minutes to midnight on Tuesday, May 16. Adrian immediately contacted bookies William Hill asking, 'Having been a fan of both the dam and sire during their racing days I wondered if you could lay me prices on the colt to win the 2000 Guineas, Derby and St Leger in 1992, plus the triple crown (all three)?

Hills laid him 500–1 for each race and 5000–1 for the triple crown.

Forty customers in a Liverpool betting shop in September 1988 refused to budge until they knew the result of the 4 o'clock at Brighton, even though firemen had rushed into the shop to put out a blaze. Icecapped won the race.

When lifelong punter Jimmy Peters passed away in September 1985, bookie John Lovell, whose shop he would regularly frequent, allowed the wake to take place in his shop. 'It is the way he would have wanted to go, he spent most of his life in betting shops' said Mr Lovell.

When journalist and radio presenter Derek Jewell died in 1985, he left in his will £1000 to racing form expert and tipster Marten Julian on condition that he 'uses the sum to be wagered on four horses of his choice.' Julian's bet raised £300 profit, and obeying the terms of the will 90% of the winnings were donated to the Injured Jockeys Fund.

When tragic pensioner Jack Martin committed suicide, he left his pal Al Morgan a betting slip for a well fancied horse in the 1985 Champion Hurdle, with a note, 'Sorry Al, matey, hope this brings you more luck than me.' It didn't; the horse, Browne's Gazette, swung round at the start of the race and was beaten.

Punters searching for supernatural inspiration may be interested to learn that The Gambling and Spirituality Workshop claim considerable success for their winner-finding method. Meeting weekly in London the group is an offshoot of the Company of Astrologers and they use that 'science' to come up with their selections. Says their leader, Maggie Hyde, 'We don't allow anyone to join who hasn't got a grounding in astrology.' Although they claim to find plenty of winners they are a little reticent about their success or otherwise. 'We don't keep books,' says Maggie Hyde.

A Torquay rugby player celebrated winning £300 on a horse by attending a local party, during the course of which he was showing off his winning betting slip when a fellow party-goer challenged him to eat it. He did so, washing it down with a pint of bitter. When he went along to the bookies to explain what had happened they refused to pay him out because he could not produce his original slip.

Injured on his way to the races, Ian Maxwell Scott refused the police offer to take him for hospital treatment until they had first taken him to a telephone kiosk so that he could ring through his bets to his bookie.

Bookies William Hill thought the punter who had written to them might have genuine 'inside' information. 'Sir, I placed a bet with you in one of your offices on Thursday, June 1' he wrote in 1978. 'I'm sorry to say my copy is lost in prison where I'm serving a long sentence. I have been sending out bets by the "back door" over the past sixteen months. As you will know I'm breaking prison rules and security so I cannot give you my name and address. I have been in prison since 1968 and I'm not due to be released until 1985 so there is no way at present that I could go to your office to fill in a claims form for my winnings. I would be grateful if you could let the person whose name and address I will supply, act on my behalf to receive any winnings if you decide I should receive them.' He was paid.

A punter backed a winner with a forged £50 note in a betting shop in Splott, Cardiff. The manager called the police who let him collect his winnings, deducted fifty quid to recompense the shop then arrested the punter.

An American punter had his honesty acknowledged in a unique manner. The track where he became the one and only punter ever to return the money he had been overpaid on a tote bet marked the occasion by staging a race in his honour.

A group of Irish punters on their way to the Cheltenham Festival races in 1986 decided to follow the signs marked HR for Horse Racing. They got hopelessly lost and ended up in Chepstow - HR stood for Holiday Route.

Just as the punter placed his bet on a horse called Deep Trouble in the Stockton-on-Tees betting shop in March 1986 a car crashed into the shop!

Punters who fancied Peter Scudamore, the champion jump jockey, to ride a treble at Chepstow on March 27 1989, didn't have much to show for their bets when he duly obliged - for the first two winners were returned at odds of 1–7 and the third was in a walk-over.

Film star Walter Matthau consulted his doctor, R B Chesne, about his general state of health, and was given a tip for the 1986 William Hill Cambridgeshire. Matthau won £2000 for £200 when Dallas won the race and said, 'I have the man who keeps me alive to thank for making me back Dallas.'

The Earl of Cork lost 'a new beaver hat' which he staked on the outcome of one of the earliest recorded Irish horse races, held at the Curragh in April, 1634 between horses owned by the Earl of Ormond, whose horse beat Lord Digby's over four miles.

In 1874 the second Lord Vivian dreamed that The Teacher had won the City and Suburban race, but when he went through the list of declared runners he could not find one of that name. He subsequently discovered that one of the runners, Aldrich, had been known as The Teacher the previous season. He bet £30 on the 33–1 outsider and won himself £1000 when the horse won by a neck.

One of the strangest of all Derby gambles took place on 500–1 outsider El Mighty in 1967. After the the *News of the World* reported a reader's vivid dream in which El Mighty was the winner, the money poured on the horse whose odds dropped until he was sixth favourite in the field of 22. With just two furlongs to go, El Mighty was heading the field, but he gradually dropped back to finish 18th, much to the relief of bookies throughout the country.

Apparently, the Scots have been great punters for many a long year - an 1863 volume, *A History of Racing* records that during the reign of King James VI, 'they became possessed of such a furious spirit of gambling that it was found necessary to restrain their passion for the sport and betting upon it, and a law was passed that no person should win more than one hundred merks, the surplus being declared to the the property of the poor.' The law was passed in 1621 - perhaps it should be reintroduced!

John Scholes of Batley remembers his most coincidental winning bet. John's father who lived in Morley, Yorkshire, used to go racing or to the local betting office every day. His Christian names were Albert Henry. Fourteen years to the day after he passed away, a horse called Albert Henry ran, in April 1988.

Albert Henry was number 14 on the race card.
It was 14 days since Albert Henry had last run.
It was quoted at 14–1.
John Scholes staked £14 on Albert Henry.
The horse didn't come 14th – it won.

Chris Liveras was so certain that his new purchase was a future Grand National winner that before it had even jumped a fence in public he backed it to win the National in 1987, 1988, 1989, 1990 and 1991. Time is rapidly running out for Mr Liveras, whose horse, Mr Chris, actually made it into the National line up in 1989, only to fail to get round. Mr Liveras staked £100 each way for each of those years at odds of 200–1, and is still hoping to get lucky.

Extremely optimistic – that's the gentleman from Paignton in Devon who asked to remain nameless, but who placed a bet in 1989 that the horse Golden Freeze, trained by Jenny Pitman would win two Cheltenham Gold Cups between 1989 and 1994 at odds of 20–1; that the horse would win three Gold Cups between 1989 and 1994 at 100–1; that the horse would win four Gold Cups between 1989 and 1994 at 500–1; that the horse would win five Gold Cups between 1989 and 1994 at 2000–1, and that Golden Freeze would win all six Gold Cups between 1989 and 1994, at odds of 10,000–1. The horse didn't win in 1989 or 1990, but the punter, who put the same bet on for a Dutch friend, said, 'We remain confirmed Jenny Pitman fans.'

A more conventional bet, but perhaps from just as optimistic a source came from the patient in a Liverpool hospital who wrote to William Hill in 1985 asking them to place a bet for him and enclosing as payment a cheque for £220 made out to the bookmakers – issued by the Department of Health and Social Security! Hills never did discover how the punter had managed to persuade the Department to make out a cheque to a bookmaker.

BOOKIES

The following is a jaundiced opinion of the Turf expressed in 1853. At the time, it was not an uncommon point of view. The year is memorable for the enactment of legislation prohibiting the free-wheeling off-course cash betting trade which flourished at the time.

'Without doubt there are many noblemen and gentlemen of high honour yet on the Turf,' wrote Harry Hieover, a sporting writer of the day, 'but the great preponderating number of mere adventurers, and regular legs (*bookmakers*), has driven almost all chance of success by fair betting off the course . . . Desperate characters, without money, and devoid of principles, bet largely on a concocted race. If fortune favours the nefarious transaction, so much the better for them; if they lose, they are still safe, for they become levanters, i.e. they abscond.

'There is little dependence to be placed now on the goodness of any horse, or on the fair conducting of most of our modern races. The horse may be drugged, or the jockey may be bribed; so numerous are the villainous practices resorted to when the favourite is heavily backed to win.

It has been asserted by a well-known rider and owner of racehorses, deep in Turf secrets, that "If Eclipse were now here, and in his very best form, but heavily backed to lose by certain influential bettors, he would have no more chance to win than if he had but the use of three of his legs." '

The first bookmaker to offocially operate on a racecourse was a Mr Ogden, who began operating at Newmarket in 1795.

Mid Glamorgan is the part of the UK best catered for in terms of betting shops with 3.41 per 10,000 population. The worst is Cornwall with 0.78 per 10,000.

A Bath bookmaker has devised a bizarre fund-raising event. Brian Halter, manager of a betting shop in the town, came up with the Shout At Your Boss Day during which his staff were allowed to yell abuse and complaints at him in return for donations to a worthy cause. Now Brian wants to extend his scheme throughout the betting and racing industry. 'It would help clear the air and raise money for charity. It could be followed by a nationwide Shout At The Customer Day, so that people who serve behind betting shop counters could be rude back to those customers who are annoying.'

A betting shop manager lost his appeal against unfair dismissal. Hardly surprising, returning from a lunchtime tipple he had bombarded staff and customers with cream cakes.

Racecourse betting attracted more than its fair share of undesirable characters in the mid-nineteenth century but even so, the incident of murder on a course witnessed and reported by repespected journalist of the time, James Greenwood, must have been a rarity. It occurred in 1868 at Alexandra Park when a bookmaker tried to make off without settling his debts. Wearing 'a black wide-awake cap with the regular betting-man's pouch slung at his side' the man was being chased by an angry crowd which dragged him to the ground. He was up again, however, 'without his hat and his face a hideous patch of crimson, but hustled towards the gate, plunging like a madman to escape the fury of his pursuers; but the policeman blocked his way and they caught him again and some punched his face while others tore his clothes.' Again the man struggled free and might have escaped had not another bookie felled him with a well aimed stool which brought him down again where he was again set upon. Finally, a mounted policeman intervened and 'the poor tattered wretch, ghastly white and streaming with blood, was hauled out and dragged away insensible, with his head hanging and his legs trailing in the dust, amid the howling and horrible execrations of five thousand Englishmen.' Fearing a riot the police hid the man in a cellar before smuggling him away under cover of dark. A couple of days later the local paper reported 'The unfortunate man who so rashly roused the fury of the sporting fraternity at Alexandra races is dead.' No-one was ever charged.

John Sebine walked into his betting shop to place a bet for pal, John Hunt, a pensioner. At home Hunt was delighted to see his horse winning him £25 and awaited Sebine's return with delight. When Sebine returned he had to tell his friend 'Sorry, I had to lend your money to the bookie.' For when John Sebine walked into the shop in Harehills, Leeds, it was to find a big queue of winning punters and a distraught manager with no cash to pay them. 'I felt sorry for the punters and lent the shop manager every penny I had on me – £70 in all, including the tenner I should have put on John Hunt's 6–4 winner.'

Racetrack tote clerk Rey Gallegos was left sweating when he inadvertently punched up a £7850 ticket for a punter who had asked for a £785 bet. The punter refused to buy the ticket, leaving Rey responsible and sweating on a debt for which he would have been responsible as the runners at the track in Florida were under orders and there was no time to cancel the bet. A couple of minutes later Rey was £31,037 richer as the favourite beat a 37–1 shot to land the winning forecast for him.

When a town decided to launch a modern day version of the game Happy Families, marketing a set of playing cards featuring such local worthies as Mr Drew the artist, Mr Crews the boatman and Mr Pillar the builder, they were pleased to include Mr Michael Blewitt the local bookmaker. The cards raised cash for a local appeal in Dartmouth.

Were bookmakers Surrey Racing looking to 'scalp' their clients when they offered odds for the World Hairdressing Championships in 1988?

Bookmakers William Hill bet regularly on the outcome of the

World Black Pudding Championships and once sponsored the World Snuff Championships.

Those same bookies were offering very generous odds about American athlete Steve Prefontaine to win an Olympic medal - unfortunately the miler had been dead for a number of months.

Special prizes for the best turned-out horse in a race are commonplace, but when bookmakers Backhouse sponsored a race at Bath in September 1989, they decided to do something different - and offered a prize for the best turned-out owner!

Bookmakers must have been laughing all the way to the bank when a horse trained by Irishman Paddy Mullins came home to win a big race at odds of 20-1. The horse was unfancied, having recently been beaten at odds-on in a two horse race. Stewards accepted Mullins' explanation that he had no explanation!

Very few punters were tempted by the world record shortest ever odds of 10,000-1 ON offered in Italy when Lester Piggott partnered Dragon Blond to win the 1987 Premio Navigio in Milan.

In 1967 William Hill laid an ante-post bet at what must have been the longest odds ever - seventy-five yards long, to be precise. A client of the bookies took out a multi-selection bet on a number of races, staking £5000 in all and making nearly two thousand separate individual wagers which had to be converted into an ante post voucher by the company. He received through the post a 225 feet long voucher crammed into a large envelope. Not one of his selections won.

TIPSTERS

The most flamboyant tipster ever to grace a racecourse was undoubtedly Prince Ras Monolulu, who was born in Abyssinia in 1880, named Peter Carl Mackay by a preacher in America, and came to England in the early twentieth century. Invariably clad in exotic, eccentric clothes, decorated with lucky charms and ostrich feathers, the Prince sought fame and fortune by screaming out his catch-phrase, 'I gotta horse' and selling racegorers his tips. Like all tipsters he had his ups and downs, but he really hit the headlines when he publicly tipped the 100-6 shot Spion Kop, who won the 1920 Derby. His heyday was between the Wars and he died in 1965 aged well over 80.

Phil Bull, who passed away in 1989, was the man who did more than perhaps any other single individual to provide punters with comprehensive, meticulously researched information about racehorses, via his Timeform service. However, but for a remarkable change of direction by his father, Phil might well have ended up in the Salvation Army, rather than leading the punters' army. Bull's father, so legend relates, was a captain in the 'Sally Army' who would chalk messages on walls in a bid to educate the local populace into the ways of the Lord. He inscribed on one such wall the slogan 'What shall we do to be saved?' only to later find someone had written underneath: 'Back Doricles for the St Leger'. This he did. The horse won at 40–1 and the Salvation Army lost a captain.

Undoubtedly a great jockey – but Lester Piggott's tipping abilities seem to leave a little to be desired. He was employed to give selections on a telephone service in 1989, but after seven weeks he was dropped. Tony Fairbairn, managing director of the service, told the *Daily Mail*, 'We found that it was very costly to keep advertising the service and, frankly, we weren't making any money out of it.'

'Find Daddy a winner', Steven Bell asked his 14-month-old daughter Shelley in June 1985. The Blackburn baby did better than that – jabbing a pen at the racing page of Steven's paper she pointed out four winners, and won him £1330.

Finding winners usually requires dogged study of the form-book, which was literally the way a Mr RKKVerschoyle of London W13 once hit the jackpot. 'I had an Irish setter dog called Sacha. I was studying the form in the *Sporting Life* one morning when Sacha jumped on me, tearing the paper. A colleague at the office suggested jokingly that he was trying to give me a tip. So we looked through the day's runners to see if there was a horse which he might fancy. We found two – Sacha's Song and Dogwalk. Just for a laugh I placed a £1 win double on the pair. They won won at 16–1 and 25–1, returning over £400. Sacha had steak for dinner that night.'

DEAD CERTS

The punters who made Demons Begone the 13th horse to have over a million dollars wagered on him for the Kentucky Derby were soon made aware of their fate. The horse, carrying $1,182,918 of public money, was pulled up on the back stretch after suffering 'an unusual bleeding problem'.

Starlite Night was reckoned to be such a 'good thing' for a race at Nottingham in July 1985, that no bookmakers would offer odds for the race. Starlite Night finished fifth of six.

Pentland Javelin, mistakenly given 21lbs less than his correct weight for a Redcar handicap in September, 1984, looked the proverbial 'blot on the handicap'. Pentland Javelin finished tenth of fourteen.

The runner at Sydney's Rosehill racecourse in 1989 looked to be a divine tip. On Water, by Godswalk, was being ridden by Kevin Moses. It finished last.

BIZARRE WAGERS

Jockey Jem Robinson landed a bizarre wager in 1824 by betting that in one week he could ride the winner of the Derby and the Oaks and get married. He won the Derby on Cedric, the Oaks on Cobweb and married Miss Powell, to win the wager.

Soccer star Stan Bowles did too much gambling and joined Gamblers

Anonymous, but he was kicked out when he started betting on how long he could stay with his therapy group.

During the mid-19th century the Duke of Richmond, who hated writing letters, was called upon to produce many of them during the course of his business. He sent one in which the message consisted of just two words to Mr Rusbridger, his land agent. On the strength of this missive, Mr Rusbridger bet a friend, John Kent, trainer of the Duke's racehorses, that he could produce the shortest letter in existence. To Rusbridger's surprise, Kent accepted the wager, and won it when he produced a letter he himself had just received from the Duke, which read 'Kent - Yes. Richmond'!

Turf raconteur Jeffrey Bernard tells a marvellous betting tale about trainer Richard Hannon in his book, *Talking Horses* (Fourth Estate). 'About ten years ago his wife had triplets, two boys and a girl. One night after his wife and children had gone to bed, Richard was downstairs enjoying a drink with a merry band of lunatic punting Irishmen when he had a brilliant idea. He crept upstairs, got hold of the triplets, brought them down to the sitting room and arranged them on the sofa. "Now," he announced "we're going to play Find the Lady." So there were the triplets gurgling happily on the sofa while all around them Richard's Irish friends were bunging on ten pound notes, twenties, fifties, until finally a fortune had piled up on each of the babies. Then Richard would remove their nappies with a flourish and pay the punters who had found the lady.'

Jockey Harry Atherton Brown caught a 44lb salmon to land the first part of an odd bet in 1921. To win the bet he had to catch a salmon and win a race within an hour. Minutes after catching the salmon, Brown raced in a chase at Hereford, and was ten lengths clear coming to the last fence when his horse fell.

Tom Scott, described as a popular local sportsman, caused a sensation in Liverpool in 1870 when accepting and winning a wager by jumping, without a horse, one complete circuit of the Grand National course.

Newmarket racecourse was the venue for the 1831 attempt by George Osbaldeston to win a 1000 guinea wager with Colonel Charrite that he could travel two hundred miles on horseback within nine hours. Using a team of 28 horses he did it in 8hrs 42mins.

Racing fan Terry Nichol decided that the small matter of getting married wasn't going to get in the way of his hobby. So the 37- year-old Trowbridge man arranged the ceremony, in September 1983, within sprinting distance of a betting shop. Terry dashed in and out of the shop before, during and after the ceremony. His wife, Janet, said, 'I don't mind as long as he keeps winning.'

Racehorse trainers Alec Stewart and Jamie Toller, plus assistant trainer Chris Thomson Jones and Teddie Beckett of the British Bloodstock Agency took on a strange bet - the stake was that the first of the four of them to become engaged should buy the others dinner in the restaurant of their choice. Stewart became engaged to Katherine Domvile, whom he wed in 1986, and had to fork out £1500 to wine and dine his pals at Le Pavillon on the Champs Elysees in Paris.

OFF COURSE

SPORT

Jim Dooler, who received a licence to train on the Flat in 1989, is a former Rugby League international.

Oliver Sherwood had soccer trials at Southend and Charlton Athletic before scoring as a jockey and trainer.

Former English Open Champion at table tennis on five occasions, Chester Barnes is now assistant to trainer Martin Pipe.

Jockey Eddy Harty, who rode Highland Wedding to victory in the 1969 Grand National was a member of Ireland's three-day event team at the 1960 Olympics in Rome.

Jockey Harry Wragg made a mark in a couple of other sports. He was a ten-handicap golfer and scored three holes-in-one, two at Newmarket and one at Doncaster. He was also a keen amateur boxer, once boxing an exhibition bout with World Bantamweight Champion Teddy Baldock in 1934. Wragg was floored in the first.

QUALIFIED

Trainer Dr Philip Pritchard of Gloucester is a qualified anaesthetist.

Former champion jump jockey Bob Davies boasts a BSc from Wye Agricultural College.

Doctor Jon Scargill, PhD, graduated from University College, London, with a first class honours degree in biochemistry before moving to Cambridge for a further three years research work for his doctorate. In 1988 he became a racehorse trainer.

MUSIC

Irish trainer Dennis Cordell-Lavarack topped the pop charts in the sixties when, under the more groovy name of Denny Cordell, he produced hit records like 'Go Now' by the Moody Blues, 'A Whiter Shade Of Pale' by Procol Harum and 'With A Little Help From My Friends' by Joe Cocker.

Trainer Geoff Huffer used to be a member of the pop group Mungo Jerry, whose 'In The Summertime' was a massive hit; and trainer Richard Hannon used to be a member of the Troggs, of 'Wild Thing' fame.

Or so they tell me – but none of the pop music books confirm the story, so what do the trainers themselves have to say? 'Richard was not a member of the Troggs and did not appear on any of their records' claimed Hannon's Wiltshire yard, while queries to the Huffer HQ in Newmarket produced a deafening silence. But a mutual friend swears it's true!

One racing personality who definitely was a member of a group is Roger Wright, Racing Editor of the national news agency, Press Association. Roger, a dab hand with a harmonica, was a long-haired member of Thackeray, who never hit the big time, but toured with David Bowie and Jethro Tull.

TELEVISION

Jonjo O'Neill appeared in TV advertisements for milk in 1981.

Willie Carson was a regular on TV's *Question Of Sport*.

Former Royal jockey Dick Francis is now a successful thriller writer.

Richard Pitman and Jimmy Lindley are TV commentators, as is Brough Scott, also an author and journalist.

Kelly Marks, female jockey, appeared in the James Bond movie *Octopussy*.

ACTORS

Trainer Dan O'Donnell, who in 1989 left his Lambourn stables to train in Macau, is a former actor who appeared in *The Greatest Story Ever Told* and *El Cid*. He also trained for the Shah of Iran.

In the early 1920s, reigning champion jockey Steve Donoghue played the hero in the film *Riding For A King*.

Bernard Dillon, who rode Flair to win the 1000 Guineas in 1906 and Lemberg to win the 1910 Derby, married music hall star Marie Lloyd in 1914.

DON'T GIVE UP THE DAY JOB

Jump jockey Andy Orkney took time off from making a spectacle of himself on British racecourses to take spectacles to villagers in Cameroon, West Africa. Optician Andy, who went at the request of Operation Raleigh, for whom he had previously worked in Peru, dispensed a thousand pairs of glasses whilst he was away in early 1989.

Jump jockey Bill Smith, who later rode regularly for the Royal family, was nearly lost to the sport, having become so homesick during his early days at the Fred Rimell stable that he returned home to Hayling Island, where he worked for eighteen months in the local branch of Moss Bros.

Irish jump jockey Anne-Marie Crowley is also a model.

Champion jump jockey Peter Scudamore used to work as an estate agent.

After his retirement, French jockey Yves Saint Martin cashed in on his well-known name by launching his own range of sunglasses, featuring his monogram at the top of one lens.

The favourite recreations of some current trainers make interesting reading:

Ian Balding
Anything fast and dangerous
Michael Blanshard
Archaeology
Henry Cecil
Gardening
Frankie Durr
Sailing
Josh Gifford
Cricket
Robert Hartop
Homeopathic treatment of horses
Clive Holmes
Mountain climbing
J P Kavanagh
Conversation
Gay Kindersley
Folk songs
Stan Mellor, MBE
Four dogs
Martin Pipe
All sports
Jenny Pitman
Watching Dallas
Sir Mark Prescott
Breeding Old English game fowl
Gordon Richards
Scuba diving
Brooke Saunders
Restoring antique furniture
Michael Stoute
Cricket

As do the favourite pastimes of some of today's jockeys:

James Akehurst
Tropical fish
Mark Birch
Crosswords
Julie Bowker
Training with St Helens rugby team
Dermot Browne
Eating
Kevin Darley
D.I.Y.
Hywel Davies
Sleeping
Trevor Davies
Running marathons
Bruce Dowling
Women
Richard Fox
Organic gardening
Steve Horsfall
Moto-cross
Alan Jones
Boxing
James Kinane
Art
Carl Llewellyn
Eating puddings
Thomas McGivern
Drinking whisky
Charles Mann
Strip poker
David Nicholls
War games
Martin Pepper
Playing guitar
Brendan Powell
Remote control car racing
Dominic Cockram
Archaeology
Teresa Elwell
Egyptian PT

Derby-winning jockey Walter Swinburn took on racing commentator Julian Wilson for a sidestake of £2000 and lost. To collect, Wilson beat Swinburn in a best-of-three toboggan race down the famed Cresta Run at St Moritz.

Jockey Hywel Davies and his wife Rachel are such great fans of the Aussie soap series, Neighbours, they named their baby daughter Kylie.

A company launched a brand new line in racing souvenirs - cushions decorated in jockey silk colours. Upstairs of Sudbury, Suffolk were charging £65 for the cushions in June 1989 - well, the stuffing is all pure feather and down.

Elliott Robertson Ltd of Harrow, North West London, launched a line of limited edition prints showing horses' racing, breeding and family history. They started with Chief Singer and branched out from there, increasing their range with personal stud books and stud cards plus personalised posters of horses showing them crossing the winning line, along with hand-scripted details of their achievements.

TURF TRIVIA

Steeplechasing was popular in Ireland in the late 18th century, but it could be a little hazardous at times, as one Colonel Yardley who raced in a chase at Kilkenny later recalled: 'During one of the races the open ditch, built up with dry gorse, was fired either by accident or design. The horses approached it in a sheet of flame, getting through with falls and considerably scorched, and one of them whose jockey pluckily remounted won the race. I have further cause to remember the meeting as my racing breeches etc were purloined.'

Racing was taking place at Ayr at least as long ago as 1576. *The History of Ayrshire Families* by a Mr Paterson records that in that year, 'My Lord Cassillis and his friends having an appointment at Ayr at a horse race, Kerse also being present with some adherents, a quarrel occurred between the parties about breaking of the drum used, no doubt, in starting the horses. A fight ensued in which John Kennedy, of Penquhiren, was shot through the leg and James Crawford was shot in the thigh, whereof he was lame all his days.'

Trainer Colin Tinkler believes that too many races are named after dead people, so when he decided to sponsor a race at Redcar he called it 'The Very Much Alive Marie Tinkler Stakes' in honour of his wife, Marie.

The largest museum in the world devoted to showcasing the Thoroughbred and the racing industry is the Kentucky Derby Museum, located adjacent to Churchill Downs, US.

Sweet Sauce was a most versatile horse. During the summer of 1860 the horse won the Stewards Cup over 6 furlongs and two days later won the Goodwood Cup over 2 miles 5 furlongs. In August 1973, Threadbare won over hurdles, over fences and on the flat on consecutive racing days.

The first horse-race trophy? It is believed to be the Silver Bell, raced for at Lanark in Scotland. In 1661 it was referred to in an Edinburgh publication as having been 'instituted by King William about 600 years since.' King William reigned from 1165 to 1214.

W Claude Motion, one time President of the New Zealand Racing Conference raced his first horse at the age of 16 and his last at the age of 92.

William Christie, who died in 1962 at the age of 103 could claim to be the oldest recorded owner - he had horses until the age of 99.

When did the winner finish seventh in the Derby? In 1896, when The Winner finished 7th in the Kentucky Derby.

Steve Cauthen's thousandth winner was called Thousandfold.

When was Second first? At Johannesburg in 1881 when the horse of that name won the first ever Johannesburg Turf Club Handicap.

When did Good Friday fall on Boxing Day? At Wolverhampton in 1899 when the horse of that name fell in the Thorneycroft Chase on Boxing Day.

What was the significance of the victory of Blanchland at Newmarket in 1886? The horse was Fred Archer's last winning mount.

In 1930 the owner-trainer-jockey combination of JJ Corry, Tom George and Jim Ellis won the first four races at the Nelson, New Zealand meeting with four different horses - Croupier, Cessation, Johneen and Kozan.

One-eyed horses have been banned from racing in Australia for over thirty years on safety grounds.

Barnsley permit-trainer Sue Plowright lectures in Law at Sheffield University.

In 1738 a meeting held at Newcastle staged a race for donkeys, who had to be ridden by chimney sweeps carrying brushes.

Desert Orchid's owner Richard Burridge co-wrote the screenplay for the movie of the Frederick Forsyth thriller *The Fourth Protocol.*

Novelist Ian Fleming, who invented James Bond, was Brough Scott's godfather - he didn't invent Scott, too, did he?

The Queen pop group topped the album charts with the LP, 'A Day At The Races' in 1977.

Top fifties jump jockey Johnny Gilbert would walk the course before racing and mark the best ground with lollipop sticks.

Little Lady won the last two furlong race for yearlings run under Jockey Club rules, in 1857.

The oldest registered colours in racing - pale yellow, or straw - belong to the 11th Duke of Devonshire, Andrew Robert Buxton Cavendish, who owned Park Top. The 1st Duke was a founder member of the Jockey Club.

In 1980 Richard Maponya became the first black racehorse owner to register his colours in South Africa. He opted for green, black and gold, the colours of the then banned African National Congress (ANC).

Perhaps the most unusual colours in racing belong to Lord Westbury - patchwork with red cap. His son, trainer James Bethell, has them specially made in Hong Kong: 'They are composed of lots of tiny squares and look exactly like a patchwork quilt.' They were originally the colours of Lord Westbury's grandfather back in the 1920s.

Newmarket vet Norman Tebutt treats injured racehorses with the Chinese art of acupuncture.

Known as the 'racing vicar', the Rev Bob Greaves used to ride around his Chaddleworth, Berkshire parish on a failed racehorse, Sportola, given to him by Robert Sangster, and which he would mount from a headstone in his churchyard. Many trainers attended his funeral in mid-1989.

Pursuing his method of earning a living, notorious pickpocket George Borough was arrested at Enfield races in 1870 and sentenced to seven years transportation to Paramatta in Australia, where he eventually became Chief of Police.

After telling everyone the good news about his huge win on the horses in 1988, New York punter Parmjit Singh was devastated to receive a phone call demanding a $350,000 ransom for his kidnapped wife. In fact Singh was something of a Billy Liar, and hadn't won the cash at all. The police soon tracked down his missing wife - she hadn't been kidnapped but had cooked up a plot to defraud her husband of his 'winnings' with her lover.

Headed for the Cheltenham National Hunt Festival, Peter and Mary Phillips were surprised to see fellow passengers on the plane they joined at Dublin clad in summer gear. Just as the plane began to rumble up the runway the penny dropped - they were on a plane bound for Las Palmas. Peter and Mary leapt to their feet and managed to have the plane stopped so that they could get off and join the right flight.

Racegoers used to being charged up to £100 a night for a room when they visited the Festival were offered accommodation with a difference in 1989 - at the local Roman Catholic convent. Nuns at La Sainte Union de Sacre Coeur convent opened their hostel to the racegoing public at £17 per night including breakfast as part of their efforts to raise money to repair the roof. 'Guests are not allowed to drink in the rooms or bet,' said one of the 12 sisters at the convent, adding, 'But it is their choice if they gamble at the races.' She also confessed to having once had a bet herself. 'The horse fell. I think my vocation steers me from such things.'

Low flying jets were blamed for causing the death of a potential Derby winner. Mrs Irene Pearson of Thimbleby, North Yorkshire, owned an eight-year-old mare called Sabhia, who was terrified when two jets, flying at only 150ft, roared above her. Mrs Pearson told the *Daily Express* in September 1989 that Sabhia then smashed through wire and wooden fences before coming to a halt with her foreleg almost severed. A vet put Sabhia out of her misery and delivered a two-weeks premature foal, whose grand sires were 1973 Derby winner Mortson, and Relko, the 1963 winner. The colt died two days later. Mrs Pearson said, 'We realise pilots of military aircraft have to train, but they should never be allowed to get away with this sort of conduct.' The Ministry of Defence said they would consider a claim for compensation, but military aircraft have not been the only guilty ones. In 1986 a £100,000 foal died at David Cecil's Helmsley stud after being frightened when three hot air balloons passed overhead.

As recently as 1985, frustrated readers of the papers provided by the local public library in Greenock, Scotland were unable to read the racing pages. For the library janitor carefully blacked them out with an ink pad and roller. The practice had been going on since the last century when, explained a spokesman for the Libraries Association, 'the blacking-out was an attempt to keep people away from gin palaces and racing'. Chief librarian Joy Monteith, who could hardly believe it was still happening, said, 'I'm mortified. The practice seems to have been carried on unthinkingly.' Said a library local, 'We had to hold the papers up to the light and read through the ink.'

Jump jockey Graham Bradley revealed his pet hate in the racing world to the *Sporting Life*: 'Izal toilet paper in the weighing room. We want Andrex.' To his surprise, within a

week he received eight rolls of Andrex, courtesy of four nurses from Milton Keynes, complete with a poem which they had written for him.

'Graham, as nurses we cope with stress and strife,
So we'll help with your pleas in the Sporting Life.
You poor old chap, how you must suffer
When an everyday task becomes rougher and rougher.
Each day you go to work, riding round and round,
You always stand up. Don't you ever sit down?
Are you different from the rest, there's always one,
Now your secret's out, Graham, you've got a sore bum.
A soothing rub with talc and oil could prove a big issue,
So, we girls have whipped round and sent you soft tissue.'

It was signed, Liz, Carole, Ann and Sue.

Reading lorry driver Ray Goddard has an unusual hobby - he collects hair from top racehorses. 56-year-old Ray has been at it since he was 13, and amongst the horses who figure in his odd collection are Indian Skimmer, Shergar, Sea Bird II, Nijinsky and Brigadier Gerard.

Racing journalists Willie Lefebvre (Press Association) and Steve Boggett (*Sporting Life*) collect metal racecourse badges. They have them from all current racecourses, and many now-defunct ones like Bogside, Lewes, Hurst Park and Lanark.

Jockeys could become redundant if Charles McVean of Tennessee gets his way. He has invented a form of racing in which remote-controlled jockeys race on Hackney ponies - half the size of a thoroughbred and a tenth of the price - in indoor arenas. 'I have the hottest property here in Memphis since Elvis Presley,' boasts Mr McVean.

NOT-SO-FAMOUS RACES

Perhaps the only race in the world where the runners are much better off if they finish second is the Kiplingcotes Derby, run near Hull since 1519. First prize is the interest from money invested by a benefactor last century, which is currently about £20, but the second prize is made up of the sum of the entry fees, which is invariably much more. The race is run over a four and a half mile farmland course.

One of the most famous, or infamous, races of all time took place at Newmarket in 1709. Racing in the north and south of the country was carried out separately in those days and the north sent down their champion, Merlin, to take on the best the south could offer, a horse nominated by King William III's 'Keeper of the running horses', William Frampton. There was vast interest in the match and unprecedented betting. The south thought they were home and dry when, in a pre-race trial, Frampton's horse finished just behind Merlin even though it had secretly been given seven pounds overweight to carry by Frampton. Unfortunately for the south, Heseltine, the northern trainer, had also over-burdened his horse by the same amount in the trial and Merlin duly won the race. Fortunes and estates were believed to be lost and anti-betting legislation passed shortly afterwards was probably introduced as a direct result of this race.

In the early days, horses weren't raced before the age of five. In those days, the official birthday of horses was May 1, today it is January 1. Gibscutski was the first two-year-old to race in public, beating a six-year-old in 1769. Three-year-old racing was first held at Beldale, Yorkshire in 1731 and four-year-olds raced for the first time at Hambleton in August 1727. Yearlings actually raced for a couple of years from 1786 but it didn't last long, although the last public yearling contest took place in 1859 at Shrewsbury.

At Lincoln in 1744 a huge crowd turned out to watch an extraordinary 14-mile race between a six-year-old and a twenty-one-year-old horse for a prize of 100 guineas. The younger runner won by a mere length in 39 minutes.

It was estimated that £100,000 was riding on the outcome of a famous £1000 a side match between Antinous, owned by the 3rd Duke of Grafton and Herod, owned by the Duke of Cumberland, in 1764. The match was run at the Beacon Course, Newmarket, and Herod won by half a neck. On one occasion the Duke, Prime Minister from 1766 to 1776, decided that he would like to drive from his home in Euston, Norfolk, to the races at Newmarket over grass. So he ordered an avenue of trees to be planted along the eighteen mile route. However, the avenue had to stop six miles short when it transpired that the Duke had overlooked one little matter – he didn't own the land.

In 1776 at Epsom, records a contemporary report, a horse was in the lead when, 'Just before he came in at the winning post, being crossed by a gentleman on horseback, the rider was thrown; but his leg hanging in the stirrup, the horse carried his weight in, and won miraculously without hurting his jockey.'

Handicap races enable horses of unequal ability to take each other on, with the weight they are carrying designed in theory to result in the horses running a dead-heat. The first public handicap race of more than two runners was at Ascot in 1791, the Oatlands Stakes.

Over £250,000 was reckoned to have been bet on the outcome of the 1799 clash between Hambletonian, winner of the 1795 St Leger and the top Northern horse, and the pride of the south of the country, Diamond. The race was run at Newmarket for a stake of 3000 guineas and Frank Buckle got the hot favourite Hambletonian home by half a neck.

Perhaps the most unsuccessful race meeting of all time was held at Kelso in 1803 when the four day meeting attracted just three runners. Every race was a walk-over.

In 1805, a race was run at Tralee in Ireland, whose conditions were advertised as being 'restricted to those who have been caused to pay out at least £200 in adverse litigation'. The race was run for a Plate donated by 'the Gentlemen of the Profession of the Law in the County of Kerry' and was won by a Protestant clergyman, the Rev Mr Denis of Wicklow.

In 1817 the Irish racing authorities decided to launch a race of their own to rival the popularity of the English Derby. They called it the O'Darby and ran it at the Curragh, but it only survived for 8 years.

The four mile steeplechase for gentleman riders at Lismore, Ireland in January 1819 must have been entertaining for spectators. Each of the four runners fell at least once and the winner fell no less than four times!

In the 1820s a series of races, including one at Goodwood, were run in which a weight allowance was given to riders who wore a cocked hat.

Epsom's Great Metropolitan Stakes, run over 2¼m, has strong claims to be considered the first sponsored race. Prize money for the first running in 1846 came from publicans and the race became known as the Publicans' Derby.

The Woodlawn Vase, the trophy for the Preakness Stakes, the second leg of the American triple crown, is reckoned to be the most valuable trophy in American sport. Its history goes back to 1860 when it was made by Tiffany & Co for the Woodland Racing Association. After being awarded for a number of events it was won by Thomas Clyde, a director of the Maryland Jockey Club, who presented it to that board in 1917 when it was first awarded for the Preakness. In 1953 Alfred Vanderbilt won the Preakness when his Native Dancer triumphed, but he refused the responsibility of looking after the Vase, which is now kept in the Baltimore Museum of Art while a half-size reproduction is awarded to Preakness winners.

The Australian Derby, run for the first time in the spring of 1861, continued every year until 1978 when a decision was taken to move it from spring to autumn. When it reappeared in autumn 1979, it was awarded to Dulcify on the disqualification of first-past-the-post Double Century. The race also featured the appearance of the first lady jockey to compete, New Zealand's Linda Jones whose mount Holy Toledo had already won the Kiwi Derby. Incidentally, with their different seasons, the spring Derby was run in late September or early October, the autumn one at Easter.

Jim Buchanan, who rode Mahutonga (1904) and Master Delaval (1906) to victory in the Auckland Cup in New Zealand, boasted of seeing 78 consecutive runnings of that race.

A British military force in Tibet in August 1909 organised a race meeting, including a steeplechase and an Army Cup – it took place in front of a bemused crowd of Nepalese, Tibetans – and four important local Lamas.

When the Duke of Portland's Roche Abbey won the Singleton Plate at Goodwood in 1909 it finished so full of running that it continued to gallop on up the slopes of nearby St Roche's Hill, where it deposited its jockey on the ground before disappearing over the brow of Trundle Hill. The jockey was unable to weigh in, since the saddle which he should have been carrying had been last spotted heading towards the Hampshire border. At the same course in 1952, Aquino II, well fancied for the Goodwood Cup, refused the urgings of his jockey to race and strolled into a nearby field where he settled down to watch his rivals toil away for over two miles.

A day at the races turned to tragedy at Royal Ascot in 1930 when a fierce thunderstorm caused the death of a Mr Hobein from Southport, struck by lightning as he sheltered under a bookmaker's umbrellas.

In 1955 two racegoers were killed by lightning during another violent thunderstorm there – one of them a pregnant woman. The meeting had been postponed from its normal date until July only because of a rail strike.

One of the most baffling and intriguing racecourse incidents occurred in the 1956 Grand National. Riding Devon Loch for the Queen Mother was jockey Dick Francis, and the pair had jumped the last clear and were striding up the run in to the finish line when, with just fifty yards to run, the horse 'fell flat on his belly, his limbs splayed out sideways and backwards in unnatural angles,' in the words of his jockey. ESB. went on to win the race but no-one has ever satisfactorily explained what happened to the Queen Mother's horse. Dick Francis concluded, 'What happened to Devon Loch is Devon Loch's secret, and I doubt if even he remembered it afterwards.'

Trainer Reg Akehurst was convinced there was a sinister and unusual reason for the disappointing performance of his Loh in the 1976 2000 Guineas – he reckoned the horse had been doped with marijuana.

All four runners came to grief at the final fence of the Chilton and Windlestone Working Men's Club Handicap Chase at Sedgefield in September 1989. Favourite Grange Of Glory actually finished on top of the fence while Invisible Thief fell just before the jump; Clonroche Stream ran into Invisible Thief and unseated his jockey, and Hatsu-Girie refused to jump upon seeing the mayhem ahead

of her. Jockey Andy Orkney literally dragged Grange Of Glory off the top of the fence, remounted, and went on to win the race.

Punters weren't taken in when the world's fastest horse made his racecourse debut – they backed his one opponent down to 14–1 ON to beat him! Which isn't quite as silly as it sounds, for nine-year-old Klute, whose speed of 44.91mph over half a furlong is an equine world record, is a non-thoroughbred and was making his first racecourse appearance when he raced at Haydock in August 1988 against modest sprint handicapper So Careful. The race was over five furlongs and So Careful stormed home by 25 lengths, leaving Klute's owner and jockey Lesley Bruce saying, 'There's something wrong with him, he's been ill.' Logically, though, the race was a mis-match along the lines of sprinter Carl Lewis taking on an 800m specialist like Sebastian Coe over the latter's favourite distance; there could only be one winner.

Jockey Lindsay Charnock didn't exactly curry favour with Indian racegoers when he lost on an odds-on favourite in Calcutta – he nearly sparked a riot. 'My horse struck the front, but then just dug his toes in and pulled up with me. I got beaten half a length and it didn't help matters that the winner was ridden by an English jockey, Terry McKeown,' said Charnock, recalling the incident in the winter of 1989. 'The crowd were going mad and I needed an escort of twenty coppers to get to the weighing room. The stewards realised what had happened, but things had become so heated, with people throwing things, that they had no option but to make the race null and void. If they hadn't given them their money back the crowd would probably have burned the stand down,' Charnock told the *Racing Post*.

The 1986 Caulfield Guineas race in Australia made history when Abaridy won it at odds of 250–1, the longest price recorded in a feature event.

Punters and racegoers alike were baffled when, during the July meeting at Killarney in 1989 the scheduled 8pm race was run at 7.30 and the scheduled 7.30 at 8pm. It later transpired that the order of running had been wrongly printed in the racecard.

On July 5, 1989, *The Times* reported: 'Hundreds of angry Greeks set fire to racetrack stands and betting offices after an outsider won a horse race in Athens.'

In April 1985 at Beirut's Palace of Peace race track, the horses lined up for the start of the third race. Suddenly, four of the most fancied horses fell, leaving a 9–1 long shot, Commodore, to romp home. Hundreds of disgruntled racegoers swarmed onto the track, trampling over fences and tearing down the display board. After fifteen minutes of bedlam it was announced that the race was void, all bets would be refunded. The decision enraged a man who had staked eleven dollars on the winner. He threatened to blow up the track if he didn't get his winnings. He was thrown out. Minutes later a rocket propelled grenade fired by an unidentified gunner hit the track.

The runners for the 2.15 race at Beverley in May 1989 had to wait in the paddock until a bullock could be removed from the course. In July 1988 the start of the Ulster Derby at Down Royal was delayed while a flock of sheep was cleared off the track.

Friday the 13th duly lived up to its reputation in 1989 when, in one of the most bizarre incidents ever seen at a major racetrack, jockey Brian Peck suffered a compound fracture of his right forearm when his mount collided with a deer in the fourth race, at Turfway Park in Florence, Kentucky. Peck, a last-minute substitute for Jack Neagle aboard Top Booking, was maintaining a two-length lead over the field down the backstretch when a buck and a doe ran from the infield across the track just past the 5 furlong pole. The buck crossed safely but the doe ran straight into Top Booking, flinging Peck into the path of the other 11 horses. Miraculously, Peck was only brushed by one other horse as the field spread out to avoid him. As Top Booking fell, his bridle flew off, getting tangled on the left foot of jockey Euclides Vergara, aboard Siesta Sunset. Vergara reached down with his left hand and grabbed the bridle, carrying it to the finish line to

ensure that other horses wouldn't get entangled. Peck was operated on, and had to have two pins and a steel plate inserted into his arm. He was expected to be out for at least two months. The horse and, apparently, the doe were uninjured. Track workers searched for the doe but were unable to find her. In addition, there is no truth to the rumour that Turfway Park has placed 'Caution, Deer Crossing' signs along the racetrack.

Jill Harmworth from Oxford couldn't decide just what to buy her husband Kenneth to celebrate his 65th birthday in July 1989 – so she plumped for a race of his own. Which is how the £4000 Harmworth Handicap came to be run at Leicester on July 10.

There were two runners for a special race at Copenhagen's Klampenborg racecourse in October 1986: five-year-old sprinter Miami Prince and Danish Greyhound Derby-winner Irish Jackpot. They raced over 450 metres and Irish Jackpot won by eight metres, leading from the start although the horse was making ground towards the finish.

The National Association of Local Government Officers trade union, NALGO, sponsored the card at Market Rasen in August 1989 and the races had names like the Help Your National Health Service Amateur Riders' Novice Hurdle and the Put People First Juvenile Novice Hurdle.

Three of the four runners fell in a flat race at Waipu, Hawkes Bay, New Zealand in 1940. Two of them were promptly remounted by spectators, who completed the course to fill the minor placings.

There was something a little unusual about the fourth finisher in the 2.15 at Lingfield on December 21, 1985 – it was a greyhound. Yankee had been at the races with owner Mrs Violet Cohen of Hove when he suddenly decided he could do better than the 17 horses legitimately entered. Said Mrs Cohen's husband, Sid, 'He dragged my wife off her feet and broke the leash. Poor Vi collapsed with shock and didn't see Yankee overtake most of the field to finish fourth.'

Four-year-old filly Sweetwater Oak clipped the heels of eventual winner Current Lady as she took part in the first race at Albany, California, in 1989. The incident sent her jockey, 19-year-old apprentice Nate Hubbard, hurtling over his mount's head to end up dangling from her neck. The stewards ruled that as Sweetwater Oak had carried the proper 113lb weight across the line and as Hubbard had not touched the ground, the horse could retain second place. Said Nate, 'I just tried to hang on so I wouldn't get run over.'

Irish jockey Mick Morrissey set out riding a 20–1 shot, and ended up riding the hot favourite. It happened at Southwell in 1953 when Morrissey partnered Knother in a two mile chase. Five fences out he crashed into the back of fallen favourite, Royal Student. Morrissey was shot high out of the saddle – and landed on Royal Student's riderless back as the favourite was getting up after his tumble. Morrissey duly jumped the last four fences on Royal Student, bringing the horse safely home, albeit in last place.

Despite hundreds of victories in the sport's most glamorous and prestigious races, when asked to name his Greatest Ride, Lester Piggott plumped for The Maltster, who he rode to victory in a £1500 race in South Africa in November 1975. The horse had beaten eleven rivals despite being left some twenty or thirty yards behind the field when the starting stall failed to open properly.

The Kentucky Derby is one of the few races to have an official beverage - the mint julep, which is a powerful concoction including in its ingredients fresh mint and the finest Kentucky Bourbon.

American Bill Shoemaker is perhaps the most successful jockey ever, but he probably still has nightmares about the 1957 Kentucky Derby when, aboard Gallant Man, he stood up in the saddle after forcing his mount ahead of Iron Liege, only to suddenly realise that he had mistaken the sixteenth pole for the winning post. Shoemaker realised his mistake, dropped back down and went for his whip, but it was too late and Iron Liege held on to win by a nose.

Jockey Greville Starkey completed a remarkable Derby-Oaks double in 1988, but you'll search in vain for a record of the feat in any form book. For both races took place at Port Elizabeth in South Africa, and both were open only to Ostriches! The Ostrich Derby and Oaks were organised by South African jockey Michael Roberts, who persuaded Walter Swinburn, Tony Ives and Bruce Raymond also to compete. But it was Greville who stole the glory while Walter Swinburn took a crashing fall shortly after the start of the Derby and excused himself from the Oaks, claiming that he'd be safer tobagganing down a mountain-side (see page 115).

Argentinian jockey Gomez, riding Epsom Lad in the 1901 Eclipse Stakes, felt the horse's saddle slip as the race progressed. Thinking quickly Gomez finished the race in first place, holding the saddle in his hand.

The author wishes to record his thanks to the many people involved in the racing world who took the trouble to supply him with information, to clarify points of contention and to suggest new contacts.

Obviously a book of this anecdotal nature derives its material from a myriad sources too tedious to itemise. Where possible I have tried to credit the sources of stories. These have ranged from 200-year-old newspapers to an enormous number of books, both ancient and modern, taking in along the way trade press and the unlikeliest of sources - amongst them a 'gentleman's magazine' perused, I hasten to add, purely in the cause of research!